BASKETBALL'S
GAME CHANGERS

Icons, Record Breakers, Rivalries, Scandals, and More

BRENDAN PRUNTY

GUILFORD, CONNECTICUT

An imprint of Globe Pequot

Distributed by NATIONAL BOOK NETWORK

British Library Cataloguing in Publication Information Available

Library of Congress Cataloging-in-Publication Data

Names: Prunty, Brendan, author.
Title: Basketball's game changers : icons, record breakers, rivalries, scandals, and more / Brendan Prunty.
Description: Guilford, Connecticut : Lyons Press, An imprint of Globe Pequot, [2017] | "Distributed by NATIONAL BOOK NETWORK"—T.p. verso. | Includes index.
Identifiers: LCCN 2016042877 (print) | LCCN 2016045063 (ebook) | ISBN 9781493026982 (hardcover/paperback) | ISBN 9781493026999 (e-book) | ISBN 9781493026999 (ebook)
Subjects: LCSH: Basketball—United States—History. | Basketball—United States—Miscellanea.
Classification: LCC GV885.7 .P78 2017 (print) | LCC GV885.7 (ebook) | DDC 796.323—dc23
LC record available at https://lccn.loc.gov/2016042877

♾™ The paper used in this publication meets the minimum requirements of American National Standard for Information Sciences—Permanence of Paper for Printed Library Materials, ANSI/NISO Z39.48-1992.

Printed in the United States of America

CONTENTS

INTRODUCTION
The Evergreen, All-Inclusive Sport

The invention of basketball was not an accident. It was developed to meet a need. Those boys simply would not play 'Drop the Handkerchief.'

—James Naismith

More than a decade ago, when I was in the process of choosing a college, I started to think about basketball. This might seem like a strange thing for a 17-year-old on the precipice of one of the most important decisions of his life to be weighing, but it's true.

Looking at schools big and small, I wondered just how good their basketball teams were. Football was too big and all-consuming. Basketball though, was intimate. It was a community atmosphere, whether you went to the University of Kentucky, which worships basketball as a religion, or New Jersey Institute of Technology, which often needs a prayer.

I finally settled on Saint Joseph's University, which straddles Philadelphia proper and the posh Main Line. The basketball history on Hawk Hill was rich—from Jack Ramsay to the Guokas family to Mike Bantom to Marvin O'Connor, to well, when I arrived. The Hawks had produced college and NBA coaches by the bushel, and pro players on occasion. They had had their moments throughout history, but never truly captured what they should have been. When I stepped on campus in the fall of 2002, the team was supposed to be good—but expectations were tempered.

Six months later, we were in the NCAA Tournament.

The next year, the biggest news to happen to the program since "Jack Ramsay hired as men's coach" came: Jameer Nelson would return for his senior season. The abridged version of what happened next is that it was the first domino in what would be a historic season for our school. The team would finish the regular season with a 27-0 record, Nelson would be an All-American, featured on the cover of *Sports Illustrated*, and the Hawks would receive a No. 1

seed in the NCAA Tournament for the first time in school history.

We attended almost every game—from the season tip-off win over Gonzaga at Madison Square Garden to the soul-crushing loss to Oklahoma State at the buzzer at the Meadowlands. ("John Lucas II" is still profanity in my presence, for the record.) In between was the greatest ride a sports fan could experience: We lived in a converted dorm house fewer than 50 yards from center court of Alumni Memorial Fieldhouse that year, were the official Delonte West fan club (The Wild Wild West—"Keepin' the peace, one dunk at a time!"), and were the heart of the student section night in and night out.

How basketball has changed from the game as played here, at Western High School, Washington, DC, circa 1899.

The point of all of this backstory is to lay the groundwork for a tale that cuts to the heart of what basketball is—and can be—from pro sports cities, to college sports towns, to asphalt playgrounds. A story that could only happen in a sport like basketball, and at a place like tiny Saint Joseph's University at the corner of 56th Street and City Avenue.

During the final week of the 2003-04 regular season, Stanford—the only other undefeated team in the land—lost to Washington on a Saturday night. St. Joe's, already having completed its season, would be ranked No. 1 when the new Associated Press Top 25 polls came out two days later. The school I screamed for every night was the No. 1 team in the country—ahead of Duke and Kentucky and North Carolina and UCLA and every other school.

That week was our final one before spring break, so we did what we normally did on weekday nights after class; we went to the gym to play a pickup game. Our small school had only a handful of courts in the rec center to play on, and all were full. One of the student attendants told us we could play on the Fieldhouse court.

Center court?! Surely, there must be some catch. There was not.

So there we were, playing five-on-five full-court hoops against some other students, fully ensconced in the game, when the doors opened. In walked the men's basketball team. We all froze. This is it. *This is where I get expelled and have to inform my mother that I have to find a new college because I played on the court reserved for the NO. 1 TEAM IN THE COUNTRY!* Head coach Phil Martelli led his squad into the gym, and as they lined up along the sideline, a friend meekly stammered out: "Uhh, s-s-s-sorry. You guys can have the floor."

Martelli looked at his watch.

"Nope," he said. "We're not on until six o'clock. You guys have another five minutes."

The No. 1 team in the country—the only remaining team in all of Division 1 without a loss to its name—had just ceded its practice floor to a bunch of scrubby sophomores jacking up far-flung 3-pointers and attempting mindless behind-the-back passes.

Only at a school like Saint Joseph's. Only in the sport of basketball.

Why bring that story up? Why tell an anecdote from my college years in a book chronicling the history of basketball? Surely, being able to play on the home court of the No. 1 team in the country is not on par with the formation of the NCAA Tournament, the institution of the 3-pointer, or the once-in-a-generation talent of a Michael Jordan. No, of course it's not. What it does show, is how basketball—this incredibly complex, yet simplistic game of firing a ball at a suspended hoop—can welcome you in like few sports can.

When given the task of putting together this book, it seemed like an arduous one: Come up with the 50 most important or influential game changers in the history of basketball? You could go on forever!

Unlike baseball, which is steeped in over a century and a half of history, or football, which ties much of its identity to a made-for-TV mythology, or hockey, which is as history rich as baseball—just most of it coming from our neighbors to the north—basketball's evolution has been a slow one. The college game reigned supreme for much of the first half of the century, then the NBA took hold, only to find that America wasn't keen on its professionals battling drug abuse as frequently as man-to-man defenses. Only in that aftermath did basketball as we know and enjoy it today—both professional and college—come to exist. Magic and Bird. A 64-team NCAA Tournament. Gender and sexual barriers being broken. The game growing globally like no other sport. All of that had to be addressed here. But if you went with the headline-making events, you might miss something critical to the evolution of the game at a micro level. So Chuck Taylor sneakers and *The White Shadow* are listed alongside John Wooden and the shot clock.

In creating what would become the final list of 50 game changers, I tried to use a simple criterion: Did it change some aspect of how the sport is viewed today?

It is why alongside the creation of the WNBA, you will see David Halberstam's classic book of basketball reporting, *The Breaks of the Game*. Why Red Auerbach has a spot on the list, as does a once-dismissed arcade game, *NBA Jam*. This book is juxtaposition of old-school and new-school. Current and former. Pretty much every key development in the game of basketball since Dr. James Naismith first nailed up a peach basket inside a rickety gym in Springfield, Massachusetts, in 1891, is represented. (And if you're wondering why Naismith isn't on this list, simple: He created the game. By definition no person, event, or innovation could become a game changer until after Naismith's initial moment of inspiration, so he is ineligible for inclusion in this book.)

There will certainly be some quibbles of course, and that is part of what makes books like these so much fun. You can argue that Wilt Chamberlain should be ranked higher than Michael Jordan. Or that Geno Auriemma should be on the list instead of Mike Krzyzewski. Or that the 1975-76 Indiana Hoosiers undefeated national championship team merits a spot instead of the Fab Five. It is the nature of sports debate. If we expanded this book to 100 game changers, someone would be outraged that something was left out.

After whittling it down to 50, the hardest task was ranking them properly. I honestly can say, I don't know if I have it correctly. Ask me in a week, and I might change the order. Ask me in a year, and I almost certainly will. It's nearly impossible to rank so many people or moments that each played a vital role in the evolution of the game. And in basketball—more so than say, baseball or football, each of which was loaded with technological innovations throughout its years—this was a list that was more personality-driven. With all due respect to the inflating needle, basketball's pretty much been the same since Day One—ball goes through hoop, team scores point. Rinse and repeat.

So you might see some of these rankings and be puzzled why someone as important as Phog Allen could be ranked behind the 1985 NBA Draft Lottery. You could make a case for either, truthfully. My advice: Treat the rankings as chapter numbers and this book as a collection of the 50 biggest game changers in the sport, randomly thrown together and told for your enjoyment.

After all, that's what it's about: The enjoyment of the game of basketball. It's why we watch the NBA Finals every year, fill out a bracket, and become invested in teams like Butler and George Mason, why we are amazed when someone pulls off a slam dunk over a car, and misses a 3-pointer to win it all.

Few sports can be as easily accessible as basketball. Baseball is pretty straightforward: throw ball, hit ball. But at a certain point, the ball is thrown faster than you can hit it and—poof!—there go those major-league dreams. Football is, too: throw ball, catch ball. But at a certain point, the guys hitting you between the throw-ball/catch-ball parts get a little bigger and a little faster and—crunch!—there go those pro dreams.

But basketball has always been an evergreen sport. You can see it, play it, and study it, whether you're eight years old or 80. It's why rec leagues around this country see kids streaming into overheated grade-school gyms on January mornings to play and learn the game. And why you'll see 50-year-old lawyers catching the early bus home to make it to their weekly game at the Y. At a certain point, it doesn't matter that you can't dunk or aren't tall enough, or jam your finger every time you go for a rebound—there are others like you willing to suffer the humiliation of trying to throw a ball through a suspended hoop.

But basketball, at its core, is a game of respect, where the law of the court is the only law that holds sway.

It's why Michael Jordan—at age 54—still thinks he can honestly beat players half his age.

"If he can do it . . ."

Take for instance, your humble author: If given the opportunity to play, I will always pick up the ball and head on to the court. But glory? No, that will never happen. I know my limitations and they are that I am 5'9" without any semblance of a vertical leap. I can guard you pretty well, pass the ball OK, and out-muscle you for a rebound every now and then. But a decent player, I am not. Still that never stopped me from picking up the ball and trying to find that Larry Bird stroke.

That is why that day on the main court at Alumni Memorial Fieldhouse on the campus of Saint Joseph's University was such a unique moment. Such an *only-in-basketball* moment. My ragtag collection of friends and I were not equals of the men's basketball team. They were 27-0. We were probably down 0-27. But basketball, at its core, is a game of respect, where the law of the court is the only law that holds sway. We were there first, we still had time left on the clock, so they waited.

Does this happen at Kentucky or North Carolina or Duke? Likely not. To play on the floor at Rupp Arena or the Dean Dome or Cameron Indoor Stadium, you've got to prove you were first worthy to walk the same pieces of hardwood as the greats that came before you. At Saint Joseph's—a small Jesuit university, with a humble persona and a blue-collar attitude—there were no dues to be paid. You had a ball and nine other players, so you had a game, regardless of what court you were on.

As we resumed that day with the No. 1 team in the country watching—no, *judging*—our every move, there was a sense of normalcy. Maybe not for us, but for them. This was a team of 20-somethings who, before the season started, were just another very good basketball team. Throughout the course of an undefeated season, they became great, instant celebrities on their own tiny campus. But here *they* were, watching us, another group of 20-somethings playing the same game, on the same floor, as they did nightly.

President Barack Obama, along with members of Congress and Cabinet secretaries, could be found jockeying for rebounds on the White House court during his time in office.

For one five-minute window, the No. 1 team in the country—the first team in 13 years in college basketball to finish the regular season without a loss—was the equal of 10 college kids darting around a gym floor, trying to play a complex, yet simple game. We eventually settled back into a rhythm, with shots made and missed. The team of All-Americans and future NBA draft picks became just another group of college kids waiting for a pickup game to finish. It was all going so great, until the law of the court issued its final judgment.

Phweeeeeeeeeeeeeeeeeeeep!

Martelli blew his whistle.

"Time's up, fellas."

THE ABA
The Black Sheep That Forced the NBA to Change—Then Made It Better

When it came, the end was swift. The American Basketball Association had been sputtering along for its last two years, struggling to draw fans and attract attention, like a car long past its expiration date. The final season of 1975-76 saw the league begin with 10 teams, but between October and May, four had folded operations. It was over. The party that had been so grand, so opulent, so one-of-a-kind, was coming to an end. Owners lamented over what could have been. Players wondered what was next. The league that the ABA had pushed and poked and prodded for nearly a decade became its savior in many ways.

NO. **5**

That's how the ABA ended.

How it lived, though? Oh boy, is that ever a story.

"It was always a little crazy—simply because of the financial situations of some teams," said Len Elmore, who played for the Indiana Pacers during its ABA days, from 1974 to 1976. "But it was all so fun because you knew you were competing against some of the greatest players. That was ultimately borne out in '76 when the merger occurred and you took a look at the (NBA) all-star teams. You took a look at who led in scoring, rebounds, assists—they were all ABA guys."

For nine glorious years, the ABA was the antidote to boring, plodding basketball. Or more succinctly: It was the antidote to the NBA. When the league began in 1967, the idea was to force a merger with the NBA. Potential owners interested in buying or starting an NBA franchise were going to be burdened with incredibly high costs and demands. In the ABA, you could get or start a team for half of what the NBA was asking. The league started, taking off with 11 teams in cities all over the country—near or in the vicinity of already-established NBA markets, and in some cases in new ones altogether.

An ABA battle for a rebound at the Nassau Coliseum in Uniondale, New York, May 14, 1976.

There were the Pittsburgh Pipers, Minnesota Muskies, Indiana Pacers, Kentucky Colonels, and New Jersey Americans in the East. In the West, there were the New Orleans Buccaneers, Dallas Chaparrals, Denver Rockets, Houston Mavericks, Anaheim Amigos, and Oakland Oaks. The hope was to get the league off the ground, give fans an alternative to the NBA—which most were becoming disenchanted with—and then tell the big brother league: "Hey, let's link up to save each other." It was kind of a foolproof plan. And given the ABA's business model at the outset (get attention), it looked like it might actually work.

For nine glorious years, the ABA was the antidote to boring, plodding basketball.

By 1967, the NBA was being smothered by the Boston Celtics. Red Auerbach's teams had been to the finals 10 times in an 11-year span, winning nine titles. They were dominant. Some might argue, too dominant for a league that was trying to grow in its own right through television. Plus, the Celtics were kind of well, *boring*. They were ruthlessly efficient and fundamentally sound. But they were not fun to watch if you lived outside of Beantown. Hardly anyone dunked, the 3-point shot did not exist, and most of the players in the NBA were clean-cut. In other words: The NBA was as stiff as its backboards.

The ABA, on the other hand, added a 3-point shot. (Its first commissioner, former NBA legend George Mikan, called it "the home run.") The league encouraged dunking. It stood up to—and beat—the NCAA, in challenging its "Four-Year Rule," which kept players from turning pro before the end of their senior year. Team uniforms were brightly colored. Black players could sport huge afros, while white players could wear long, moppy hair. It was a league that was completely in the spirit of the times, when America was changing and looking for ways to challenge the establishment—not just in terms of style, but style of play, too.

"I don't think the players themselves viewed it as a renegade league," Walt Szczerbiak, a player for the Pittsburgh Condors told the *Beaver County Times* in 2001. "They just wanted to play basketball. I think players like playing the ABA game as opposed to the NBA that was kind of rough-and-tumble and slow-down. The ABA was a quicker type game."

Pretty soon, players in college wised up that they could come out of college early, play professional in the United States against viable competition, and either make a career out of the ABA or wait for the NBA to take notice and jump ship. Either way, they were making money and playing good basketball at a time when they otherwise would have been playing in college for nothing. Julius Erving entered the league. Artis Gilmore did the same. Spencer Haywood—one of the most dominant players in college at the time—left the University of Detroit early to play for the Denver Rockets for a season. Haywood signed a massive contract at the time ($450,000) and led the league in scoring (30.0) and rebounding (19.5) averages.

"The eyes of basketball kind of popped open that maybe a young guy could play professionally at a really young age," Haywood told the website MassLive.com in 2015. "The next year I went to Seattle, but I had one year left on my eligibility in college. You had to wait four years after your high-school class graduated before you could enter the NBA. When I entered the NBA, I didn't realize it would be such a lawsuit that it would go on all the way to the Supreme Court. And it did. I thought it changed the game."

One of many instances where the ABA did just that.

Enjoy the Slam Dunk Contest that the NBA puts on during Saturday night of All-Star Weekend? That was the ABA's creation, too. At the time *Sports Illustrated* called it the "best halftime innovation since the bathroom." How could you not love something so flamboyant and so outlandish as a dunk contest, with players like Julius Erving—big afro, flying through the air—slamming it home from the foul line. It was classic ABA.

"We were sitting around the office one day discussing things that would draw more people, and it just came to us—'Let's have a dunk contest,'" Jim Bukata, former director for marketing and public relations for the ABA, told the *Houston Chronicle*. "That's really where it came from—three guys talking about what we could do to sell a few more tickets."

Sell a few more tickets. That was always the ABA's mindset. Unfortunately, it would also be the reason that as the league was capturing the attention of the media and NBA, it was slowly sinking into the abyss. The one thing the ABA failed to attain that the NBA had was a television contract. Occasionally an ABA game would sneak onto a local station in some fashion, but for the most part, it was a league that was spread by word of mouth. But at

On the ABA Being More than Just a Renegade League

AND ONE!

"In the end, its legacy comes down to the innovation within the sport. That's what the fans remember because it piqued their interest."—*Len Elmore, who played for the Indiana Pacers during its ABA days, from 1974 to 1976*

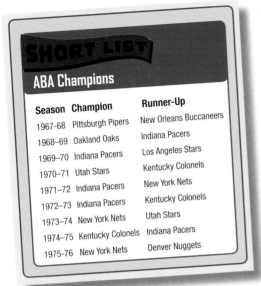

SHORT LIST

ABA Champions

Season	Champion	Runner-Up
1967-68	Pittsburgh Pipers	New Orleans Buccaneers
1968–69	Oakland Oaks	Indiana Pacers
1969–70	Indiana Pacers	Los Angeles Stars
1970–71	Utah Stars	Kentucky Colonels
1971–72	Indiana Pacers	New York Nets
1972–73	Indiana Pacers	Kentucky Colonels
1973–74	New York Nets	Utah Stars
1974–75	Kentucky Colonels	Indiana Pacers
1975-76	New York Nets	Denver Nuggets

some point, word of mouth just isn't good enough—you need to reach fans sitting at home and capture their attention. The NBA had been on television in some form since 1953. During the lifetime of the ABA, the NBA had national contracts to broadcast games with ABC and then CBS.

The ABA was left in the dark.

As a result, crowds started dwindling in many markets. From the 11 teams that started play in 1967, many went belly-up and relocated elsewhere year after year. That inexpensive buy-in that attracted so many owners became the reason it was easy for so many to throw in the towel when they saw how much money they were losing compared to what they were shelling out. When teams starting coming as fast as they were leaving, it was hard for fans to get invested when they were around.

"That was one of the reasons I signed with the Pacers," Elmore remembered. "When I signed, I had my lawyers do the due diligence on which teams were financially sound. If I had been offered to play on the Virginia Squires or some of these other franchises, I wouldn't have done it. NBA teams tried to take advantage of some of those financial problems that ABA teams were having when it came to courting players."

By the start of the ABA's final season, the signs were there that the league would not be able to survive much longer. The bills started piling up for many franchises and the numbers were adding up. On June 17, 1976, the news came out that the ABA and NBA would merge— but it would be the NBA absolving the ABA, not the other way around as the ABA once envisioned. Four franchises would be folded into the league—the New York Nets (formerly Americans), Denver Nuggets (formerly Rockets), San Antonio Spurs (formerly Dallas Chaparrals), and Pacers—while two others (Kentucky Colonels and Utah Rockies— who had recently signed a deal with the owners of the Spirits of St. Louis to move that franchise to Utah) were paid to fold by the surviving ones.

"It's better to have two teams disbanded rather than six," Larry Fleisher, general counsel of the NBA Players Association, was quoted in the *New York Times* at the time of the merger announcement. "I don't think the ABA would have been able to survive another year."

Soon the ABA collapse became the NBA's windfall. Those players that electrified the ABA became stars in the NBA. The flair and style of play that typified and defined the ABA helped make the NBA game more appealing to fans—and to television audiences. It was essentially the shot in the arm the NBA had needed for the better part of a decade. It was just so surprising it came from the entity that had been formed in the hope of taking the league over.

"I think, in all due respect to both leagues, without the merger, they both would've gone down," Elmore said. "That's why the NBA was smart enough to buy out some of the owners of the ABA."

Today, the ABA lives on in the form of the four franchises who were saved in the merger. The Spurs have won multiple titles. The Nets and Pacers have each played in at least one NBA Finals. Fans continue to clamor for throwback jerseys of Dr. J (Erving), the Iceman (George Gervin), the A-Train (Gilmore) and Chairman of the Boards (Moses Malone) as fashion statements. More so than anything else, the high-energy, entertaining style of play we see today from teams like the Golden State Warriors, Cleveland Cavaliers, and Los Angeles Clippers owes a direct debt to the ABA.

Soon the ABA collapse became the NBA's windfall. Those players that electrified the ABA became stars in the NBA.

In one last streak of brilliance, one set of ABA owners ended up being paid millions each year by the NBA in what many have dubbed the "greatest sports deal of all time." When the merger occurred, and the owners of the St. Louis franchise had their deal to sell to Utah nixed, Daniel and Ozzie Silna agreed to receive a portion of the NBA's television revenue—which as of 2015 has netted the brothers hundreds of millions.

The ABA, always with the last laugh.

Perhaps it was just too good of a show to last for that long, and all of the freedom and expressiveness came at a price. That may be true, but the merger that killed the ABA undeniably saved the NBA and paved the way for the renaissance that would come shortly after.

THE BIRD-MAGIC RIVALRY

A Battle That Defined an Era and Saved a League

It was a Friday night in Los Angeles, and the Great Western Forum was again packed to the rafters. Celebrities sitting courtside, the Laker Girls dancing along the baseline, national media crammed into tight quarters. They were all in the building for one reason: Lakers-Celtics. It wasn't what it used to be—the teams were a bit older now, the rosters changed—but the rivalry had come to define the NBA for the better part of the previous 12 years. Between 1980 and 1989, the two franchises rekindled their old clashes, accounting for eight of the 10 titles won. They met to decide the crown three times—in 1984, 1985, and 1987—with the Lakers winning two of the meetings.

On this night in the Inglewood section of Los Angeles, they were meeting for the second and final time in the 1990-91 season. That was why the place was buzzing. Because fans knew that every time these two teams emerged from opposing tunnels, history could end up happening. What no one in the building knew—not the celebrities sitting courtside or the Laker Girls or the national media—was that they were about to witness the rivalry within the rivalry for the final time.

For February 15, 1991, would be the last time that Larry Joe Bird and Earvin Johnson Jr. would face each other on the same court in an NBA game.

Larry Bird speaks to the crowd gathered at a ceremony to retire former Los Angeles Laker guard Earvin "Magic" Johnson's jersey.

"I've never seen nobody as good as him," Bird said before that would-be final showdown, as described in Jack McCallum's classic book, *Unfinished Business: On and Off the Court with the 1990-91 Boston Celtics*. "And there'll probably be nobody down the road as good as him. There's other guys who will come along who can score and rebound. But there probably won't be anybody who can control a game like he does."

"We're mirrors of each other," Johnson told the *Los Angeles Times* in 2012. "I may smile a little bit more, but the way we play the game of basketball was exactly the same because we would do anything to win. We didn't care about scoring points. We cared about winning the game and making our teammates better. That's why we were able to change not only basketball, but able to change the NBA, too."

They were the equivalent of winning the Powerball before the bank forecloses on your house. They were the equivalent of getting upgraded to first class from coach.

They were, well, the saviors of the NBA.

February 15, 1991, would be the last time that Larry Joe Bird and Earvin Johnson Jr. would face each other on the same court in an NBA game.

It all started with what is still the most-watched NCAA championship game in history. Mighty Michigan State—led by the local kid, with the flair for the big play—against tiny Indiana State—led by the farmboy with the game straight out of central casting. Magic Johnson against Larry Bird. The first battle in what would become a roundball opera for the next 15 years.

The NCAA Tournament was a big deal back then, but still had yet to have its iconic moment. Sure, there were the dynasties of UCLA and the powerhouses who still ruled the day— North Carolina and Kentucky and Kansas—but seminal moment? Frankly, none existed. The tournament was still pretty formulaic, with the general public picking up interest as the Final Four approached. But with Magic and Bird, television and sportswriters had the ultimate story to get behind. You were either a Magic guy or a Bird guy. It was David (Bird) against Goliath (Magic). And when the game tipped off, the fortunes of the NCAA Tournament went up and never came back down.

Hardly anyone remembers the outcome (Michigan State won) or the final score (75–64), but something bigger had been established. These two players had *the goods*. They were big, but could do things that bigger players and smaller players could do. Magic, was a 6'9" *point guard*. Seeing him in action in 1979, one immediately must have assumed he was created in a laboratory. Bird, also 6'9", was a master tactician, learning the weak points of opponents' games and attacking. They could pass, shoot, rebound, play multiple positions. They were, in no uncertain terms, the future of basketball.

And they were on their way to save the National Basketball Association from itself.

By 1979, the NBA was—in the minds of most of the sporting public—a circus at best, an unwatchable disaster at worst. The late 1960s and the 70s had proven to be disastrous for the league. As America underwent a cultural shift, so too, did the NBA. The clean-cut, fundamentally sound champions like the Boston Celtics were past their prime. Many fans who bought tickets and watched the games on television didn't like the color mixture the league was trending toward: black and green.

The league's racial makeup was changing, and so were its finances. Players were being paid more than ever before. And with that money came problems—mainly in the form of drugs. A 1980 story that ran in the *Los Angeles Times* cited league general managers on the record, estimating that cocaine use among players was between 50 and 75 percent. Suburban Americans didn't like paying to watch coked-out, overpaid, primadonnas play. As a result, the image of the NBA plummeted. It got so bad that even the league's own television partner—CBS—aired both Game 7s of the 1979 conference finals on tape delay. Clearly, the NBA needed a boost. Enter Magic and Bird.

Both players entered the league in the fall of 1979. Johnson had been the No. 1 pick by the Lakers, while Bird had been picked sixth in 1978, but—under the old rules—the Celtics kept his rights after he went back to college for a year. From the very beginning, it was clear that the hype that had been built around them because of their matchup in the NCAA final was well deserved. Bird averaged a double-double as a rookie (21.3 points and 10.4 rebounds), while Magic nearly averaged a triple-double (18.0 points, 7.7 rebounds, and 7.3 assists). Magic won the title his rookie year, while Bird won Rookie of the Year. Both were All-Stars. Magic would be named the MVP of the NBA Finals, and Bird would be named to the NBA's First Team.

In Bird and Magic, the league had a tandem it could sell to *everybody*. Bird would keep the fans pining for the all-white days of the league from totally turning it off (and in turn, those fans would also begin to appreciate the different style of play some black players offered). Magic presented a clean-cut image of a black player, with a megawatt smile, who wasn't a me-first athlete (and would keep black fans from thinking the league was trying to promote "great white hype" players instead of more talented black athletes).

SHORT LIST

Magic-Bird Head-to-Head Matchups, NBA Finals

YEAR	WINNER
1984	Boston Celtics
1985	Los Angeles Lakers

It was the ultimate setup for a star-driven spectacle: There was black versus white, flash versus fundamentals, Hollywood glitz versus Boston blue-collar, Lakers versus Celtics.

"But put 50 basketball minds in a room and ask them to pick a player to start their team, 25 of them will choose Bird," former NBA commissioner David Stern told the *New York Times* ahead of the 1984 Finals. "And the other 25 will pick Magic."

It wasn't a fictitious rivalry either—Magic and Bird at first, truly didn't like each other. In the first matchup during their rookie year—the first game since the 1979 NCAA final—Bird gave Magic a hard foul on his first attempt at the basket. That set the tone for the next decade of play. Two of the best players in the game, going toe to toe.

"The vibe was ugly," Johnson said in the 2010 HBO documentary, *Magic & Bird: A Courtship of Rivals*. "It was nasty. We didn't like each other."

"I just didn't want to be around him," Bird said. "That was my main competition."

What neither player knew at the time was that each was thinking the same thoughts. As the 80s progressed and it became clear that the two best players played on the two best teams, each sought motivation in what the other did. Magic would reportedly check the schedule each year when it was released and circle the two games against the Celtics. Bird would routinely check the box scores in the paper each morning to see what Johnson had done the night before. It became a game of H-O-R-S-E and the beneficiary was the NBA and its fans.

"I thought I had died and gone to heaven," Stern told ESPN in 2014. "When I became commissioner in '84, I thought what you did was go from Boston to LA and back again because it was the NBA Finals."

Stern had taken over in 1984, rising from within the league offices, and knew the tumultuous times the NBA was going through. When he inherited the commissioner's chair from

"The college game was already on the launching pad. Then Bird and Magic came along and pushed the button."
—*Al McGuire, who called the Bird-Magic NCAA Championship Game February 15, 1991*

AND ONE!

Larry O'Brien, one of his first missions was to change the image of the league. He wanted to grow its business reach, much like the NFL had done, and now he finally had his ammunition—in two great players, but more importantly, two great winners.

As the 80s gave way to the 90s, and the two gladiators saw themselves age and mature, the frostiness between the two melted away. A Converse commercial—both were endorsees of the same sneaker brand—filmed in Bird's home state of Indiana, helped break the tension between the two. Between takes, Bird got to know Earvin; Magic got to know Larry. Even though their battles in the NBA Finals and twice a year during the regular season were all business, there was now an added level of respect.

Shortly before that February 15 game during the 1990-91 season, Magic was asked to pose for a *Sports Illustrated* cover photo about the NBA stars who would be participating in the 1992 Summer Olympics. Magic said he would do it under one condition: Bird had to be on the team. Then

If Michael Jordan—who entered the league in 1984—built the NBA as we know it today, then Magic and Bird poured the foundation.

34 and with a balky back that had begun to siphon his incredible play, Bird was looking to skip the first foray of NBA players into the Games. Magic called him continually, badgering him to be a part of what would become "The Dream Team."

Bird finally relented. The iconic photo of Michael Jordan, flanked by Magic Johnson and Larry Bird, would be taken soon after the season.

By 1992, both would be gone from the NBA, Bird forced into retirement with back issues that crippled his game, and Magic suddenly—and shockingly—due to his diagnosis with the HIV/AIDS virus. When the news came out, some nine months after their final meeting on the court, one of the first phone calls Johnson received was from Bird. The two struggled to form words and thoughts and emotions. There was a bond there. That night was the one time in Bird's career that he didn't want to play. But he did, and they saw each other on the court again, first at the 1992 NBA All-Star Game, when Magic made a one-day comeback. Then, finally, as part of the Dream Team.

Magic was the ceremonial leader, with Bird as more of a ceremonial member, but they were together—finally—on the same team. And when the Dream Team made its debut at the Tournament of the Americas in Portland in June of 1992, both Magic and Bird were in the starting lineup. The opening tip landed in the hands of Magic Johnson. After a few dribbles up the court, he immediately made his first pass of the game.

It was to Larry Bird, who promptly scored.

JOHN WOODEN

Building a Pyramid of Success That Lasted a Lifetime

The unincorporated township of Hall, Indiana, still to this day has fewer than 4,000 residents. It's a tiny dot on a map, nearly halfway between Indianapolis and Terre Haute, along I-70. Though, of course when he was born here in 1910, the interstate was more than four decades away from even showing up. By the time it did, John Robert Wooden had already been in Westwood, California, for eight seasons, made the NCAA Tournament six times, and the national semifinals three times.

NO.

There simply is no way to put the legendary career of Wooden—the "Wizard of Westwood"—into the proper perspective. You're always bound to leave something out. When your career spans parts of four decades, includes 10 national championships, 12 appearances in the Final Four, countless accolades—from Coach of the Year awards, to Hall of Fame enshrinements, to personal awards for players, to the litany of great players he coached —there are few things left to say. Or even fewer ways to say them.

That the basketball universe got to enjoy the talents and grace of Wooden for almost a full 100 years is testament that he was the consummate coach. Others may have won more games, captured more championships, coached more No. 1 draft picks, made more money, or built stronger empires—but none have defined the coaching position more than the man himself.

Doubt that claim? Walk into any manager's office—we're not talking a pro sports manager, either—from a supermarket chain all the way to the CEO of a Fortune 500 company, and you're likely to find a copy of John Wooden's "Pyramid of Success."

His influence went beyond the basketball court, simply because he was so successful on it. In an era where every detail and thought wasn't available to everyone for their

John Wooden, whose influence went beyond the basketball court, simply because he was so successful on it.

consumption, Wooden's principles towered over everyone else's methods. He was so good, so efficient at what he did as the head coach of the UCLA Bruins men's basketball team for 27 seasons between 1948 and 1975, that his methods begged to be copied.

And they were. From competitors to future generations. Even when Wooden left the sidelines, he was still the godfather of the profession, a man to be consulted for every matter that dealt with the coaching of others.

"Quite likely, his accomplishments as a college basketball coach will never be matched," Duke head coach Mike Krzyzewski said following Wooden's death in 2010. "Neither will the impact he had on his players or the greater basketball community. Many have called Coach Wooden the 'gold standard' of coaches. I believe he was the 'gold standard' of people and carried himself with uncommon grace, dignity and humility. Coach Wooden's name is synonymous with excellence, and deservedly so. He was one of the great leaders—in any profession—of his generation. We are blessed that the sport of basketball benefitted from his talents for so long."

There simply is no way to put the legendary career of Wooden—the "Wizard of Westwood"—into the proper perspective.

When Wooden began his career at UCLA, the school had only had three other head coaches. Wooden, a man who had been born and raised and appeared to be set to live the rest of his life in the Midwest, had only two years of coaching experience. And that was at Indiana State, competing in the Indiana Intercollegiate Conference. Before that, he was a high school basketball coach—first, at Dayton High School in Kentucky, and then at South Bend High School in Indiana. But the seeds for greatness were already being planted. His combined record in 11 years of high school coaching: 218 wins and 42 losses. (He must have learned quickly from his first year at Dayton, where his team finished with a 6-11 record—it was the first and only time he posted a losing record as a coach in his entire career.)

But when UCLA came calling, it was not the vaunted UCLA that Wooden turned it into. The Bruins had stumbled on hard times in the 1930s and 1940s, as Pierce "Caddy" Works struggled to replicate earlier successes; and then Wilbur Johns continued the trend.

Wooden fashioned a simple, yet innovative system—still used by most coaches across all levels to this day—by putting his players in a "high-post offense" on one side and a 1-3-1 defense on the other end. The turnaround was immediate in Los Angeles. Wooden won 46 games in his first two seasons with the Bruins, and the best players in the country began to think about coming to sunny Southern California to play for his team.

Rafer Johnson. Willie Naulls. Walt Hazzard. Gail Goodrich. Lew Alcindor (now Kareem

Abdul-Jabbar). Curtis Rowe. Sidney Wicks. Henry Bibby. Swen Nater. Bill Walton. Jamaal Wilkes. Dave Meyers. Marques Johnson.

All of them—and so many more—spanned the 27-year career of Wooden at UCLA.

"It's kind of hard to talk about Coach Wooden simply, because he was a complex man," Abdul-Jabbar said in 2010. "But he taught in a very simple way. He just used sports as a means to teach us how to apply ourselves to any situation."

Abdul-Jabbar—who came to UCLA from New York City as Lew Alcindor in 1965—helped build Wooden's empire. He was the most heralded high school player in recent memory when Wooden secured his recruitment to the West Coast, snatching him from the traditional East Coast powerhouses thought to be the destination for the 7'2" teenager. But Wooden sensed Alcindor's desire for a quality education and his enthrallment with African-American culture. (UCLA had been the school of choice of Jackie Robinson, and the home to a rising black sports star, a sophomore on the school's tennis team—Arthur Ashe.) Instead of offering hollow promises, Wooden offered what he knew Alcindor was looking for—which matched what UCLA had to offer. He committed, setting up the greatest dynasty in college basketball history.

"He set quite an example," Abdul-Jabbar said. "He was more like a parent than a coach. He really was a very selfless and giving human being, but he was a disciplinarian. We learned all about those aspects of life that most kids want to skip over. He wouldn't let us do that."

Beginning with Alcindor's sophomore season in Westwood—the NCAA's freshman rule was still in effect, meaning Alcindor had to play on the freshman team for a year—UCLA established itself as the gold standard for the sport at the collegiate level. The program won the national championship for the next three seasons. After Alcindor left, people thought the dominance would end. How very wrong they were.

"Be more concerned with your character than your reputation, because your character is what you really are, while your reputation is merely what others think you are."

"A coach is someone who can give correction without causing resentment."

"I'd rather have a lot of talent and a little experience than a lot of experience and a little talent."

—*John Wooden*

AND ONE!

SHORT LIST

Wooden's Seven Consecutive Championships

1966–67	UCLA 79 Dayton 64
1967–68	UCLA 78 North Carolina 55
1968–69	UCLA 92 Purdue 72
1969–70	UCLA 80 Jacksonville 69
1970–71	UCLA 68 Villanova 62
1971–72	UCLA 81 Florida State 76
1972–73	UCLA 87 Memphis State 66

UCLA went to the Final Four for the next six seasons. It won five more national championships, bringing Wooden's total since his arrival at the school to 10—far and away the most ever for any coach. He had turned a college program into the NCAA's version of Red Auerbach's Boston Celtics—winning year in and year out. But unlike Auerbach, who had the luxury of having the same nucleus for his championship decade, Wooden was crafting magic out of a new team every year. Sure, it helped when Alcindor and then Walton—two of the best big men in college basketball history—chose UCLA, but the surrounding pieces also had to be there. And they had to work.

Wooden meshed it all perfectly.

"Coach Wooden taught by example," Walton said. "He never asked or expected anyone to do anything that he hadn't already done himself. He gave us the ability to learn how to learn, and to compete. His keen knowledge and foresight to always be about what's next, always about the future, enabled him to lead an incredibly active, constructive, positive and contributing life."

During that stretch of greatness, Wooden's team won a then-NCAA record for consecutive wins with 88. (The mark was broken by the Connecticut women's basketball team in 2010—six months after Wooden's death—with the Huskies being the only comparable dynasty to UCLA's on the college level.) UCLA posted four 30-0 seasons during the 12-year run of greatness. He even retired on top, an achievement rare among athletes or coaches. Following his final national championship–winning season in 1974-75, Wooden left the bench.

It seems almost unfathomable that during his entire nearly 30-year run at UCLA, he was never paid more than $35,000 a year and never asked for a raise. Compare that to what many high-profile college coaches earn yearly. Factor in that he once turned down an offer from Lakers owner Jack Kent Cooke to coach in the NBA for 10 times what he made at UCLA , and you get a sense of why Wooden's principles ring true to this day.

"My first four years at UCLA, I worked in the mornings at a dairy from six to noon, then I'd come into UCLA," he told the Associated Press in 1995. "Why did I do it? Because I needed the money. I was a dispatcher of trucks in the San Fernando Valley and was a troubleshooter. After all the trucks made their deliveries and came back, I would call in the next day's orders, sweep out the place and head over the hill to UCLA."

Work ethic was at the forefront of Wooden's teachings at UCLA.

He didn't permit flashy exploits on or off the court. A fancy pass in the heat of the game always resulted in a quick hook and a seat on the bench. Dunks were allowed under his eye (before they were banned by the NCAA), as long as they were straightforward and basic. And if you didn't come to practice or a game looking clean-cut, you didn't dress. Just ask Walton, who was once ordered to trim his bushy red hair. He returned from the barber with a minor clipping.

"Bill, that's not short enough," Wooden told him. "We're sure going to miss you on this team. Get on out of here."

A fancy pass in the heat of the game always resulted in a quick hook and a seat on the bench.

The star player quickly got back to the barber, got a buzz cut, and made the last half-hour of practice.

"He was always the boss," Wilkes said in 2010. "He always knew what to say. Even in the heyday of winning and losing, you could almost discuss anything with him. He always had that composure and wit about him. He could connect with all kinds of people and situations and always be in control of himself and seemingly of the situation."

The only situation that Wooden couldn't control emerged after his retirement. In 1982, the *Los Angeles Times* cracked the Wooden mystique when it reported that a booster, Sam Gilbert, had befriended a number of the program's top players from the late 1960s through the end of Wooden's tenure on campus. "Papa Sam," as he was known, counseled Abdul-Jabbar, Naulls, and Lucius Allen on various matters. He handled the pro contracts for a number of players, including Walton and Abdul-Jabbar. More damning were the allegations that he bought cars, clothes, and even paid for abortions for some girlfriends of team members.

"I warned them, but I couldn't pick their friends," Wooden told *Sports Illustrated* in 1989. "I honestly felt Sam meant well."

The accusations stung Wooden. While the NCAA never investigated, it left a permanent mark on Wooden's career resume. Those who knew him believed it to be the honest mistake of a man who was genuine and welcomed all into his kingdom. When Wooden died in 2010, the blemish was merely a footnote in his obituary. After all, one of the building blocks of his "Pyramid of Success" is "friendship."

Below that pyramid though, are what Wooden termed "12 Lessons in Leadership." Everything from keeping your emotions in check to teamwork. The No. 1 lesson that Wooden put down was the one that he lived his life by, and can be considered the defining trait of his life—and especially, his career.

"Good values attract good people."

MICHAEL JORDAN

Taking Basketball, Branding, and Business to Unthinkable Heights

Anyone who missed the signs, in retrospect, was just plain ignoring them. Michael Jordan had been destined for success. He had those unique twists in his origin story that signal greatness. There was the first (as a sophomore he didn't make the cut for his varsity team), which only served as a base for the rest. He had that second twist (he was the third pick in 1984 when he was drafted), which was a second harbinger for what was coming. He had a third (for the first third of his professional career, he was viewed as a one-dimensional player), which pegged him into a hole few players emerge from. He was destined for greatness. The signs were there, everyone choosing to ignore them along the way. But aside from the threads in the story that made Michael Jeffrey Jordan *Michael Jeffrey Jordan*, the one sign that everyone missed was an anachronistic tool delivered to the doorsteps of a couple hundred thousand people shortly before December of 1982.

It was a phone book.

More precisely, it was the Southern Bell system's Yellow Pages book for the Chapel Hill/ Carrboro region of North Carolina, which included the Research Triangle Park. The tagline at the bottom? "North Carolina is the state of champions." The photo splashed on the front cover? Michael Jordan, in that splendid white and powder blue uniform of the North Carolina Tar Heels, in the air, arms extended, the ball still hugging the tips of his right hand, Georgetown's Eric Smith beneath him, head already turned toward the basket as if he knows what's coming. This photo on the cover of this phone book is the first visual evidence that the exploits of Jordan on a basketball court could reach beyond the backboard.

Michael Jordan dunks the ball during the All-Star Weekend's Slam Dunk Contest in 1988.

SHORT LIST

Michael Jordan's Highest Scoring Games

Points Scored	Date	Opponent
69	March 28, 1990	Cleveland Cavaliers
64	January 16, 1993	Orlando Magic
63*	April 20, 1986	Boston Celtics
61	March 4, 1987	Detroit Pistons
61	April 16, 1987	Atlanta Hawks
59	April 3, 1988	Detroit Pistons
58	February 26, 1987	New Jersey Nets
57	December 23, 1992	Washington Bullets
56	March 24, 1987	Philadelphia 76ers
55	March 28, 1995	New York Knicks

* Occurred in a playoff game

Jordan was something else, something entirely different from any basketball player who came before him, and something that every basketball player who came after him would aspire to be.

"When you went to the games, you literally didn't want to miss one second because you never knew what you might miss," current Bulls COO Michael Reinsdorf—son of the longtime Bulls owner, Jerry—told a Chicago radio station in 2013. "All eyes were always on Michael and it was an incredible, joyous opportunity to get to see him play."

For nine NBA seasons (then a year sojourn playing minor-league baseball), then four more NBA seasons (then a second retirement), then two more (before finally, an official retirement), Jordan captivated the world's stage like few others before him. His talent on the basketball court was unmatched, otherworldly. From the very first time he stepped on a basketball court at Laney High School in Wilmington, North Carolina, to the University of North Carolina, to the Chicago Bulls, to even the Washington Wizards—Jordan was the ultimate of icons. His popularity and persona, both on the court and off, was measured against only two individuals: Babe Ruth and Muhammad Ali.

Jordan redefined so many things about the game of basketball that it seemed he at times dwarfed the sport he played. The second time he played on the US Olympic basketball team —The Dream Team in 1992—his presence among a gallery of superstars would send fans and other Olympians into a frenzy. He was so good at what he did, and his belief in himself was so strong, that once the winning started, Jordan was hailed as the definition of success. Here was a kid, once cut from his varsity high school team, now the man behind NBA championships, Olympic gold medals, and the most lucrative sneaker line in modern history.

"Sports is at the heart of American culture," Nike chairman Phil Knight said in a 1992 interview with *Harvard Business Review*. "You can't explain much in 60 seconds, but when you show Michael Jordan, you don't have to. It's that simple."

It was. When Jordan arrived in the NBA in 1984, he found a league that was undergoing a renaissance. The drug-addled days of pro basketball were beginning to be wiped away thanks to the exploits of Magic Johnson's Lakers and Larry Bird's Celtics. People were starting to pay attention to the sport again, which was good timing because they were about to see the greatest show to pick up a basketball. Jordan wasn't just good; he was doing things in his early years that players of his ilk just didn't do. Franchises were still building teams around centers. Jordan flipped that on its head. *You could build a future around a guard?!*

He would win Rookie of the Year and make the All-Star team and the NBA's second team. It was a precursor of what was to come. By the time Jordan walked away for good 18 years later in 2003, he had compiled an incredible career: six NBA championships (two three-peats), six Finals MVP awards, five league MVPs, 14 All-Star Game appearances (and three All-Star MVPs), NBA First Team 10 times, Defensive Player of the Year in 1988 (the same year he won the second of seven-straight scoring titles), league steals leader three times, fourth all-time in points scored, member of the NBA's 50th Anniversary team, two-time Olympic gold medalist, and even two-time Slam Dunk Contest winner.

The photo splashed on the front cover? Michael Jordan, in that splendid white and powder blue uniform of the North Carolina Tar Heels.

Many felt Jordan was the best who had ever played the game. Many still do. Bill Russell may have more titles, Kareem Abdul-Jabbar may have more points, Wilt Chamberlain may have been more dominant, LeBron James may be more complete of a player. But no one did for basketball what Jordan did during his nearly two decades on the court.

He was the first modern athlete to build himself into a *brand*. Through his endorsement deal with Nike to create the Air Jordan line of sneakers, Jordan became the most marketable commodity going. During an era when America was booming economically, no stock was soaring higher than that of his Airness. And even when the inevitable slings and arrows came his way—he's too selfish a player, doesn't treat teammates well, the gambling issues, the on-again off-again retirements—they never seemed to dent the armor that Jordan had built.

When the first series of Mars Blackmon commercials for the Air Jordans came out with Spike Lee, Jordan became a target of Hollywood. Warner Brothers built an entire cartoon movie—starring Looney Tunes characters—around Jordan's presence in *Space Jam*.

"Michael has said I helped turn him into a dream," said Jim Riswold, a copywriter for Wieden+Kennedy, the ad agency that worked on the Air Jordan campaign for Nike.

It was a dream that the NBA and the sports world used as a money tree during his career. Three years before Jordan debuted in the league, television ratings for the NBA Finals checked in at 6.7. The rivalry of Magic and Bird helped make cracks in the dam, but Jordan broke the floodgates open. By 1998—Jordan's final appearance in the NBA Finals and final season with the Bulls—the Finals achieved a still-record 18.7 rating and 33 share, meaning the series was seen by nearly 30 million households in the United States.

Jordan *became* basketball business. The league enjoyed revenues the likes of which seemed like a pipe dream in the 1970s. The NBA was able to parlay Jordan's presence—and the fans demand for him—into a massive new television contract with NBC in 1990, $601 million for four years. (NBC and the NBA would re-up four years later for $892 million, and then $1.6 *billion* in 1998.) In 2008, when the NBA Store in Manhattan unveiled its list of the most popular jerseys sold during its 10 years of being in business, Jordan's was No. 1. "Michael clearly changed the model," Jordan's longtime agent David Falk told the *Wall Street Journal* in 1998.

And to think, it all could have lasted much longer—or the very least, been more continuous—had Jordan not retired following his father's murder in 1993. That prompted Jordan, already feeling the weight of being the world's icon, to hit the pause button to chase a dream of being a professional baseball player. He spent the 1994 season riding the bus (a luxury one he leased out for the team) going from minor-league outpost to minor-league outpost with the Birmingham Barons, the Double-A affiliate for the Chicago White Sox. It turned into a familiar tune for Jordan: Critics said he couldn't succeed and was ruining his legacy. He, in turn, only pushed himself harder to prove them wrong.

"The good thing was he was eager to learn and he respected the game," Terry Francona, who managed the Barons that season, told Yahoo! Sports in 2013. "You remember back, it was really kind of fashionable to be critical of him. That really bothered me. It was anything but. He was actually very refreshing. All the things you ask of a young player, he did. He was never late for a bus. He stayed in the same hotels. It had all the makings of being a circus and it never happened. I would think for the very most part, it was because of him."

On Keeping the Competitive Fire Burning

"One day you might look up and see me playing the game at 50. [Audience laughs] Oh, don't laugh. Never say never. Because limits, like fears, are often just an illusion."

—*from Michael Jordan's Hall of Fame Induction Speech*

AND ONE!

Jordan would eventually give up baseball—in part because of the 1994 strike that canceled the remainder of the season—returning to the Bulls. He came back to Chicago with a renewed sense of purpose and passion. Jordan, who initially had a "for the love of the game" clause in his first contract (meaning he could play basketball at any time, in any setting, and the Bulls would allow it), rediscovered that part of himself by playing with baseball players chasing a dream. He saw what he loved about competing, which had gone missing through the building of *Michael Jordan*.

He would win three more NBA championships.

The legacy of Jordan has amazingly grown even after his playing days officially ended. There were some bumps along the way—much like his early playing days, when he struggled to trust teammates—for instance, when Jordan became the director of basketball operations for the Wizards. He was once again labeled as a failure and was eventually fired. But he learned. And when Jordan bought a minority stake in the expansion, Charlotte Bobcats in 2006, he came armed with lessons learned.

In 2010, Jordan . . . assumed ownership of the franchise and became the first-ever minority owner in NBA history.

In 2010, Jordan once again made history when he assumed ownership of the franchise and became the first-ever minority owner in NBA history.

"Purchasing the Bobcats is the culmination of my post-playing career goal of becoming the majority owner of a NBA franchise," Jordan said at the time. "I am especially pleased to have the opportunity to build a winning team in my home state of North Carolina."

He, of course, has done that. Renamed the Charlotte Hornets in 2014, Jordan's franchise has made the playoffs in two of the last three seasons. He's finding it's a slower process than his playing days, but once upon a time turning around the Chicago Bulls wasn't so easy either.

Jordan is in his fifties now, still as much of an icon as he ever was, still one of the most famous people in the world. He is learning that he can't control every situation on the court—though, in the back of his mind he likely believes he can still play, *and beat* today's players—but the time for being that man has passed. Each year, as a new superstar grows bigger or emerges, they are always compared to Jordan. Every title LeBron James wins dredges up the LeBron vs. Michael argument. Every point Kobe Bryant scored dredged up the Kobe vs. Michael argument. A never-ending cycle of measurements against a player to whom no one else can be measured.

Jordan was the first, coming at a time tailor-made for his success and his story.

All you had to do was be dialed-in to see it.

THE DREAM TEAM

Changing the Olympics, the Game, and Its Reach—Forever

"It was," head coach Chuck Daly said, "like Elvis and the Beatles put together. Traveling with the Dream Team was like traveling with 12 rock stars. That's all I can compare it to."

How do you measure the impact of the greatest sports team ever assembled?

Is it by the games they won? Is it by the lives they impacted? Is it by the way they made fans who came to their games feel? Is it by the medals that were placed around their necks? Is it by the legacy they left behind?

Even answering all of those questions would not suffice. Trying to encapsulate what the Dream Team meant to the world—and the world of basketball—is nearly impossible. It was a comet streaking through the sky that will never be seen again. Eleven of the best basketball players the planet has ever seen (and one who was one of the best college basketball had ever seen), coming together for the first and only time, during one magical summer showcase—which just so happened to be the biggest sports stage the world had to offer. If you weren't around to experience it, it was exactly how Daly—the man picked to coach the team—described it. They quickly became America's fastest-growing love interest and showed the rest of the world just how cool the sport of basketball could be.

The Dream Team was, in a nutshell, one of the few things in the sports universe that not only lived up to the hype, but exceeded it. "If it would've happened today, it would've been one of those reality shows," Larry Bird told *Sports Illustrated*'s Jack McCallum in his 2012 book, *Dream Team*.

From left the USA's John Stockton, Chris Mullin, Charles Barkley, and Magic Johnson rejoice with their gold medals in 1992.

Michael Jordan. Magic Johnson. Larry Bird. Charles Barkley. Patrick Ewing. Karl Malone. Scottie Pippen. David Robinson. Clyde Drexler. Chris Mullin. John Stockton. Eleven future Hall of Famers in their own right, all playing together in the midst of their absolute primes. (Christian Laettner, the consensus national player of the year in college, was the only collegian on the team. He was, and has since, been considered an afterthought among the massive collection of the legends of the game on that team.) It was a surreal thing to witness the greatest players in the game at that time, banding together to take on the Summer Olympics. But when the Barcelona games arrived in 1992, it marked the first time that NBA players would be allowed to play in the Olympics, lifting a ban that only allowed amateurs and players from other pro leagues (outside of the NBA) to participate.

. . . when the Barcelona games arrived in 1992, it marked the first time that NBA players would be allowed to play in the Olympics . . .

Once that bizarre rule was lifted by FIBA in 1989, the wheels began to turn.

While the final product on the floor was flawless and ruthless, it took a roundabout process to not only determine the roster, but to finalize it. There were egos involved and fences to be mended. Petty differences reigned supreme in some cases, causing some of the top talented players to be left off. Even when the roster was finalized, there were a number of internal squabbles that had the potential to become greater rifts—if the perfect man for the job hadn't been hired: Detroit Pistons head coach, Chuck Daly. He had been, up until May of that year, the head coach of the baddest team the NBA had ever seen. Under his watch, the "Bad Boys" Pistons won back-to-back NBA titles, with some eclectic personalities. Managing egos would be the biggest requirement for the job, and no one did a better job than Daly.

Daly had created a series of defenses during the Pistons playoff runs of the late 80s—"The Jordan Rules"—that stymied and frustrated Jordan. Yet Jordan and Daly would be almost inseparable during the run-up to and then during the Games. One of the biggest minor controversies in the selection of the team was the decision to leave Isiah Thomas off the roster. Thomas had been Daly's point guard in Detroit and was widely considered one of the best—if not *the* best—points in the NBA. But Thomas was unpopular with numerous teams, namely Jordan and the Bulls. (Thomas also fell out of favor with Johnson, after calling into question his sexuality following Magic's HIV diagnosis.) Daly removed himself from campaigning for certain players, opting to let the selection committee for USA Basketball do the work.

"If they were selecting solely on ability and accomplishments, Isiah Thomas may have deserved it," David DuPree, who covered the team for *USA Today*, told *GQ* in 2012. "But who are you going to leave off? Nobody was tougher than John Stockton; nobody was a better passer."

That was a common motif in the selection process—*who are you going to leave off?* Consider some of the names outside of Thomas's who were: Joe Dumars, Kevin McHale, Dominique Wilkins, Reggie Miller. All of them Hall of Famers. Even the runner-up in the sweepstakes for the token college-player spot on the team was one: Shaquille O'Neal.

So, the team was set. And when they convened in La Jolla, California, in June for a mini-camp of sorts, everyone was focused on two questions: *Just how hard would these guys play?* and *How the hell are the 11 best players on the planet going to share one basketball?* Ah, but Daly had it all covered. While it's true that the jaunt to La Jolla was in part a run-of-the-mill mini-camp, Daly saw it as a chance to bring the team together, as he organized the only loss the Dream Team would suffer during its existence: against a group of the nation's best college players.

"The first time we saw them, they looked like babies," Barkley told *GQ*. "We were like, 'Hey man, let's don't kill these little kids.' And they were playing like it was Game 7. Before we knew it, they upset us."

The team consisting of future NBA players—Bobby Hurley, Grant Hill, Chris Webber, Penny Hardaway, Eric Montross, Rodney Rogers, Jamal Mashburn, coached by Roy Williams—took it to the Dream Team. They won by 20. What everyone, outside of Daly, didn't know was that it was a setup. Daly *wanted* his team to lose. He took Jordan out at key times, put together matchups that he knew needed work, and so, inevitably failed when put under pressure. The point he was trying to make from the start of this whole escapade was this: *You can lose.* Message heard. The next day, the Dream Team walloped the college kids.

After qualifying at the Tournament of the Americas in Portland—where the Dream Team had to *pose for a picture* before its first game with Cuba, before destroying them by 79 points—it was off to Monte Carlo for training before heading to the games in Barcelona. At Monte Carlo,

On Dream Team Practice against College Players

"The first time we saw them, they looked like babies. We were like, 'Hey man, let's don't kill these little kids.' And they were playing like it's Game Seven."—*Charles Barkley*

AND ONE!

SHORT LIST

Points Scored—Team USA, 1992 Olympics

Charles Barkley	144 points
Michael Jordan	119 points
Karl Malone	104 points
Chris Mullin	103 points
Clyde Drexler	84 points
Patrick Ewing	76 points
Scottie Pippen	72 points
David Robinson	72 points
Larry Bird	67 points
Magic Johnson	48 points
Christian Laettner	38 points
John Stockton	11 points

the Dream Team played the famous "The Greatest Game That Nobody Ever Saw." It was an intra-squad scrimmage between Magic Johnson's Blue Team (Johnson, Malone, Stockton, Drexler, Mullin, Robinson) and Michael Jordan's White Team (Jordan, Pippen, Ewing, Barkley, Bird, Laettner).

"Everybody asks me about that game," Jordan said in McCallum's book. "It was the most fun I ever had on a basketball court."

It was also the last time the Dream Team would face heated competition. By the time they arrived in Spain for the Olympics, the city had been transformed into a Dream Team lovefest. Police escorts were needed, and news helicopters mixed with police helicopters above their every move. It seemed that the team had become bigger than the Games itself. Not everyone was happy about it, but what could you do? These were some of the biggest athletic stars in the world, all on one team.

Team USA's march to the gold medal was never in doubt. The first game against Angola (preceded by Barkley's infamous remarks at the pregame press conference: "I don't know nothin' 'bout Angola. But Angola's in trouble.") was won by 68 points. The next against Croatia, a 33-point victory. By 43 against Germany, by 44 against Brazil, by 41 against Spain to advance to the knockout stage. There they crushed Puerto Rico by 38, then clobbered Lithuania by 51 to advance to the gold medal game. In a rematch against Croatia, they had their closest margin of victory yet . . . winning by 32 points.

"It was like, the guys (Team USA) lost in '88, and so then they sent in the Navy SEALs," Ewing said to *GQ*. "We were the Navy SEALs. We were the elite forces, the elite of the elite forces. We came in, and we kicked butt and took names and got everybody back home safely."

The team had done what it was designed to do: win it all and showcase just what type of talent the USA had. Its under-the-surface effect was felt just as much. Dirk Nowitzki was 14 years old in Germany when he watched his national team get pounded by the Americans. He didn't care; he saw the beauty of the sport and fell in love. There were other ripple effects: Nene Hilario and Leandro Barbosa of Brazil watched; Steve Nash of Canada watched before heading off to college; Tony Parker watched in France; Hedo Turkoglu and Mehmet Okur watched in Turkey; in the country where the games were being held, Pau Gasol and Jose Calderon were enraptured by what they saw.

"The Dream Team was the single biggest impact of any team in any sport in history," Sarunas Marciulionis of Lithuania told McCallum. "How many kids around the world started playing? How many said, 'Oh this is a great game. Is it maybe better than soccer?'"

The basketball exhibition conducted by the United States in Barcelona that summer was essentially a free clinic for the world. Europeans were already invading the NBA game at a rapidly expanding pace, but it was mostly relegated to former Eastern Bloc countries. Now, watching Magic and Bird and Michael put on a showcase

The team had done what it was designed to do: win it all and showcase just what type of talent the USA had.

for two weeks, every kid in every country around the world with the ability to find a ball and something resembling a rim, wanted to play basketball. It turned the NBA into the first professional sports league to think globally—outside of its own continent. In turn, the international members of the game elevated their games to match the United States. Eventually the league would welcome players from Nigeria, China, Italy, and Australia as No. 1 picks, play games in Asia, Europe, and Mexico, and open offices on five continents.

"[T]wenty-five, 30 years ago in our country, a lot of people felt we were the only ones who played basketball, and that's a ridiculous thing to think," Mike Krzyzewski, a Dream Team assistant coach that year and later head coach for three US Olympic teams, said to *USA Today* in 2012. "And we don't think that way. We think it's beautiful."

It has been. In the quarter-century since the Dream Team first stepped out on to the floor, it has been lauded as one of the best ambassadorships for any sport in history. The collection of talent and personalities was the perfect blend for the global audience. While 11 of the 12 players on that team would be enshrined in the Basketball Hall of Fame when their careers ended (plus Daly, and assistants Lenny Wilkens and Krzyzewski), the entire team was inducted in 2010.

They were dubbed "the greatest collection of basketball talent on the planet."

That is undoubtedly true, but the Dream Team's lasting legacy will always be the talent that soon found itself magnetized to the sport—and eventually the NBA—after those Summer Olympics, a 20-plus-year run of players who became hooked on basketball by watching 11 of the best players ever to play the game dominating one field of teams.

Even Elvis and the Beatles couldn't claim that one.

DAVID STERN

Taking a Sport Nobody Wanted to Every Corner of the Globe—and Beyond

Upon entering the lobby of the Olympic Tower on Fifth Avenue in Manhattan, where the NBA offices are located, one would expect a display of massive proportions. A mural of Magic and Larry and Michael? Nope. Busts of Russell and Wilt and Kareem? Try Springfield for those. Replicas of the championship trophy, the MVP award? Not a one. No, the lobby of the building shows no traces of the NBA even existing. There's a waterfall on one wall, some art, statues of Greek gods (not LeBron), and some flowers planted. Mainly, there's just a lot of gray stone. Take the elevator up to the 12th floor and it only gets a little more self-serving. You can find a couple of NBA logos here and there, a mock foul lane on one of the floors, some memorabilia in a showcase here or there.

For the most part, pretty spartan for a league that made just over $5 billion in 2015, and $900 million in operating profit. A league that signed a $24 billion media rights deal in 2014. A league that has offices on five continents, in cities like London, Istanbul, Mumbai, Mexico City, and Beijing. A league that is home to three of the top-10 highest-paid athletes in contracts and endorsements in the world, as of 2016—more than the NFL, more than professional golf, more than baseball, more than international soccer.

This casual, non-assuming office space is the result of one man who came along at the right time in the sport's history, changing the way that owners, players, fans, media, and anyone else saw basketball. For under his 30-year reign atop that perch on Fifth Avenue, David Stern turned a sideshow sport into the main event.

"David knew what the perception was and in order to make it attractive to corporate America, he got a drug policy, the salary cap, and he promoted players like Magic Johnson and Julius Erving as individual players and as the best athletes in the world," Steve Mills,

David Stern at the Fortune Brainstorm TECH 2012 in Aspen, Colorado.

a former executive for the NBA for 16 years, told *SportsBusiness Journal* in 2014. "The players became the biggest assets the league had."

Before Stern ascended to the commissioner's chair in 1984, the NBA had never even considered anything of the sort. Under Stern's predecessor (and boss) Larry O'Brien and the commissioners who came before him, the NBA existed on the outskirts of pro sports in North America. It was fairly small (only 23 teams) and lagged behind Major League Baseball in cache, the National Football League in TV eyeballs, and the National Hockey League in devoted fan following.

"We were," Rick Welts, a former NBA executive under Stern, told David Halberstam for his 1999 book, *Playing For Keeps: Michael Jordan & the World He Made*, "regarded as being somewhere between mud wrestling and tractor pulling."

The NBA, though, never had a commissioner quite like Stern. He was a New York City kid, who grew up idolizing the Knicks, the son of a deli owner in the city's Chelsea section. Stern was a relentless worker, who—despite putting himself through college at Rutgers and then law school at Columbia—soaked up basketball in his free time. He would buy cheap tickets to Madison Square Garden to watch his beloved Knicks play, and then tip an usher once inside for better seats. The Knicks were terrible during his formative years, but the game spoke to Stern in a way it spoke to few others.

Once it was time to start a professional legal career, he started working for Proskauer, Rose, Goetz, and Mendelsohn—one of the premier firms in the Manhattan. Inside those offices is where his profession and his passion would cross paths. The firm had taken on the NBA as

"He's always been a hard-driving guy. Maybe he was a little easier going, again, because there was less pressure than after the NBA started growing like crazy. But he was always a very hard-working guy. He expected everyone that worked with him to work almost as hard. He always was a stickler for detail, even things that didn't seem important at the time—like exactly how you worded a memo, exactly how you worded a press release, how you ran an event."—*Russ Granik, former NBA deputy commissioner, NBA.com*

AND ONE!

a client in the 1960s, giving Stern the opportunity to work some of its cases—and come into contact with the people around the game. In 1978, he became the league's general counsel, working closely with O'Brien. When O'Brien stepped aside, Stern was the natural choice for the job—not just because he understood the business and the relationships needed to maintain and grow it, but because he knew the people and history of the game.

The NBA had been blessed with Magic Johnson, Larry Bird, and Michael Jordan right as Stern took over. He had a vision to take the sport to a global level—which seemed absurd since the league was still tape-delaying playoff games—but he instilled a cult-like mindset to make it happen.

And it did.

Jaunts to overseas destinations became the norm. Marketable stars like Jordan and Magic became global ambassadors for the sport. Stern pushed to have NBA players compete for the US Olympic basketball team, and the Dream Team exploded the sport in ways even he never imagined. Pretty soon, the NBA was everywhere: on shirts and hats, video games and TV programs, in books and magazines. Fans couldn't devour enough NBA, and Stern continued to give it to them.

Marketable stars like Jordan and Magic became global ambassadors for the sport.

"He has a great ability to see any issue from both sides," sports power-agent Arn Tellem said to *SportsBusiness Journal*. "Having empathy is an important skill in any negotiation, and even though he could disagree, one of his greatest strengths was to see it from the other person's perspective—not to say he wasn't strong-willed, but he could always grasp the other side of any argument—that is an essential skill for any deal-maker, and David is one of the best. Take all the other commissioners combined and I don't think they equal his impact."

That very well may be true. When Stern finally retired in 2014, he passed the baton off to one of his deputies—Adam Silver—to run the operation. The NBA barely even skipped a beat.

The 24-Second Shot Clock

Time, to Save the Game of Basketball

The NBA was in trouble.

Actually, scratch that: The NBA wasn't just in trouble; it was floundering. Just as the league was beginning to get off the ground in the 1950s—it had an established roster of teams, and was developing household names who would become stars—people began to tune the product out. It was boring. It had no rhythm, no feel. A game that should have been a fast-paced, up-and-down sport was becoming something else entirely. Professional basketball was becoming a high-priced game of "keep away."

NO. **7**

"That was the way the game was played—get a lead and put the ball in the icebox," Bob Cousy, the Boston Celtics legend and one of the game's best guards, said in an interview with NBA.com in the late 1990s. "Teams literally started sitting on the ball in the third quarter. Coaches are conservative by nature, and it didn't make much sense to play a wide-open game. We'd get a lead, and you'd see good ol' No. 14 [Cousy himself] doing his tricks out there."

The reason? Basketball was never designed to have—or need—a shot clock. It never occurred to anyone to introduce the feature into the game.

As the game began to get more popular, and by nature smarter people began to play it, teams began employing different methods to keep leads without having to risk giving them up. With no timed incentive to shoot the ball, teams would get a lead, and then go into passing mode. Teams would pass the ball—without being penalized—around their end of the court. Only two things could force a change of possession at the time: a turnover (which rarely happened, since pressure defense was virtually nonexistent), or a player would be fouled.

Above the backboard, time keeps on slipping.

Second halves of games would become monotonous marches from one end of the floor to the other, often with minutes of repetitive passing. (You can see how fans were becoming bored with the product.)

"The game had become a stalling game," Danny Biasone, owner of the Syracuse Nationals, said in an interview before his death in 1992. "A team would get ahead, even in the first half, and it would go into a stall. The other team would keep fouling, and it got to be a constant parade to the foul line. Boy, was it dull."

The NCAA wouldn't adopt a shot clock until the 1985-86 season.

Dull? Sure. Boring? Absolutely. Life-threatening to a game people wanted to enjoy? No question about it.

Biasone, an Italian immigrant and lover of the game, was one of the few who saw this downward trend and began to grow concerned. On November 22, 1950, a game between the Fort Wayne Pistons and the Minneapolis Lakers ended in a record low final score: 19–18. The fourth quarter score was 3–1 in favor of the Pistons. Neither team broke single-digits in a quarter throughout the course of the game.

The next year, a game between the Indianapolis Olympians and Rochester Royals lasted a (to this day) NBA record six overtimes. Sounds exhilarating, right? Not so much, as the overtime scoreline read like this: 2–2, 0–0, 2–2, 0–0, 4–4, 2–0. After the tip, either team would hold the ball until time ran out and they could attempt the game-winning shot. Fans booed mercilessly and left before the game was over.

Two years later, a game between Biasone's Nationals and the Boston Celtics had 106 fouls called and 128 free throws attempted. (Cousy scored 30 points from the foul line that night.)

Something clearly needed to be done, and Biasone had an idea he started pushing: a 24-second shot clock.

Biasone—whose main job outside of owning the Nationals was as the owner of the Eastwood Sports Center bowling alley—did some quick math to come up with 24 seconds. He looked at good, competitive games without stalling and saw that most teams were taking around 60 shots a game each. With the game being 48 minutes long, he divided 120 shots into 2,880 seconds and came up with 24 seconds, an incredibly obvious answer to a very worrisome problem for the NBA.

Red Auerbach called the shot clock "the single most important rule change in the last 50 years." Former NBA president Maurice Podoloff went a step further, saying: "The adoption of the clock was the most important event in the NBA."

So for the beginning of the 1954-55 season, the NBA debuted its new shot clock. It was an immediate success. Scoring jumped incredibly, from 79.5 points per game the year before, to 93.1 in its first season of use. Individual scoring actually dropped—the Philadelphia Warriors' Neil Johnston was the leading scorer in the league both seasons, but scored 24.5 before the clock and 22.7 in its first season. That wasn't a problem for the league, as it meant more players were getting the chance to score because the ball was being distributed more.

"It's one of those intrinsically perfect, wonderfully illogical, perfectly imperfect numbers—like nine innings in baseball and 18 holes in golf," former NBA guard Mike Newlin told *Sports Illustrated* in 1989 for a story on the shot clock's 35th anniversary. "It's an orphan number that fits perfectly into the family of basketball."

As the shot clock gained a foothold in the game, other leagues and organizations began to adopt one as well. The American Basketball League and American Basketball Association both used 30-second clocks during their brief existences. (The ABA switched to 24 seconds for its final season, however.) Women's college basketball, which was overseen by the Commission on Intercollegiate Athletics for Women, used a 30-second clock experimentally in 1969-70, before putting the clock in for good the next season.

Men's college basketball held out the longest. The NCAA wouldn't adopt a shot clock until the 1985-86 season—*more than three decades after the NBA.* Even then, it was a bastardized version, with 45 seconds being the limit until 1993, when it moved to 35, before finally settling at 30 in 2015-16.

Biasone finally received credit for the clock's introduction, when he was inducted into the Hall of Fame in 2000. But his rationale for getting the NBA to time itself seems simple, all these years later.

"If you're a promoter, that won't do," he said. "You've got to have offense, because offense excites people."

On the NBA's Early Shot Clock Days

"I remember Red Auerbach sat us down before the first game with the clock and said, 'Don't think about it.' He told us to just go out and play our game naturally. And we did. I don't think we were called two times in the entire season for not getting a shot off within 24 seconds."—*Bob Cousy,* Sports Illustrated

AND ONE!

The 3-Point Shot

Three Really Is Better than Two

 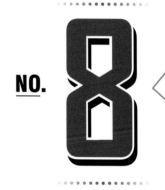

Really, when you think about it, the concept is a pretty simple one. Since its inception, a shot in basketball had always had just one valuation attached to it: two points. The game was measured by 2-point shots. If you laid it in from point-blank range? It was worth two points. If you took an 18-foot jump shot? It was worth two points. If you threw it in from 90 feet away? Yep, still worth two points.

It's a silly concept, one that now seems anachronistic. Why stick to two points? Why not assign greater value to shots that were farther away from the basket? After all, it had some risk-reward feel to it. But basketball at large wouldn't have it. It was too gimmicky. Too "playground." It didn't have a place in the modern game. The NBA, in the 1960s, certainly wasn't about to introduce a sideshow shot into a league that was finally gaining public acceptance. It had a reputation to uphold, after all.

The American Basketball Association however, did not.

George Mikan, the ABA's commissioner as the league got off the ground in 1967, needed to put butts in the seats to continue to keep the league afloat. The ABA sought to be an alternative option for basketball fans—they wanted to be everything the NBA was not. The NBA was in the midst of being dominated by the Boston Celtics. Red Auerbach's dynasty was exceptional in its stranglehold over the league, but it lacked charisma. There was nothing that jumped out at fans, who were slowly transitioning to a sports-as-entertainment society. Mikan's league had already instituted a 30-second shot clock (the NBA used a 24-second one) to promote a more up-tempo style of offensive play. He wanted to put something else into play as well.

Indiana Pacers guard Reggie Miller shoots for three over New York Knicks guard Greg Anthony in 1995's Eastern Conference semifinal.

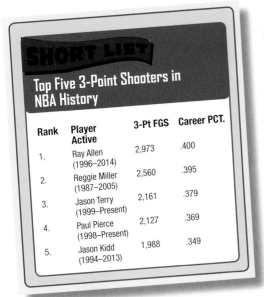

SHORT LIST

Top Five 3-Point Shooters in NBA History

Rank	Player Active	3-Pt FGS	Career PCT.
1.	Ray Allen (1996–2014)	2,973	.400
2.	Reggie Miller (1987–2005)	2,560	.395
3.	Jason Terry (1999–Present)	2,161	.379
4.	Paul Pierce (1998–Present)	2,127	.369
5.	Jason Kidd (1994–2013)	1,988	.349

He turned to the 3-point shot. "We called it, 'the home run,'" Mikan said in the 1990 book, *Loose Balls: The Short, Wild Life of the American Basketball Association*. "It brought the fans out of their seats."

The shot had been tried out before the ABA's inaugural 1967-68 season—it appeared as early as 1945, in a college game between Columbia and Fordham— but never had caught on in the mainstream. The first league to use the shot was the short-lived American Basketball League, after founder Abe Saperstein (who had run the Harlem Globetrotters) pushed for it, as a way to generate fan interest. The shot folded with the league in 1963.

Mikan revived it. And, in the run-and-gun brand of ABA basketball, it found a permanent home.

As the league gained popularity with fans, the 3-pointer became part of mainstream basketball. Louie Dampier—who had been a star at Kentucky and was drafted by the Kentucky Colonels— was the sport's first long-distance threat. In nine years in the ABA, Dampier made 794 3-pointers—almost 300 more than any other player at that time. While the shot garnered attention for the burgeoning league, it continued to have its fair share of critics. Some argued that it rewarded poor shot selection and discouraged passing offense, which had been hallmarks of basketball since the beginning. By simply running down the floor and throwing up a 3-pointer, it killed offensive creativity. So, when the ABA folded and merged with the NBA in 1976, the league pushed back at the notion that it adopt the 3-point line.

Once again, the shot was dead.

It wasn't until the 1979-80 season—three years after the league merged with the ABA— that it finally came around to the 3-pointer (though many still bristled at its inclusion).

"The NBA was rebellious against the 3-pointer at first because it was born out of the ABA," George Karl, who played in the ABA and coached in the NBA after the merger, told *ESPN The Magazine* in 2015. "For years, the NBA guys kind of said, 'That's not a good shot! That's playground basketball!'"

Slowly, but surely, the 3-pointer finally found its home in the NBA. In 1986, the NCAA adopted the shot for college basketball, which cemented its legitimization. From there, there was no turning back.

"I tell people, you look at the numbers of how many 3-pointers I made at the professional level," said Reggie Miller, who is second all-time in NBA history for 3-pointers made (2,560). "It really set up the rest of my game. Even though I made a lot of 3s, if you look at me from year two to say, year 12 professionally—my free-throw attempts, they were way up. I was setting up from behind the 3 [point line] and then going to the hole and getting fouled."

Ball screens and motion offenses no longer just set up players for open jump shots . . .

Miller's point only further underscored how far the 3-point shot had come in the game of basketball. It was no longer just a shot from long range (23 feet, 9 inches at the NBA level; 22 feet, one inch at the international level; and 20 feet, 9 inches at the collegiate level), but a tool that players were using to make the game more intricate. It was expanding precisely what its critics said it would stifle—offensive creativity. Ball screens and motion offenses no longer just set up players for open jump shots, they sprang them free for game-breaking 3-pointers. And if you could find a player who could excel at that trait—like Miller did with UCLA in college and then for 18 seasons with the Indiana Pacers—it transformed a team's offense.

"The 3 was so big for me," Miller said. "I think today, you have some guys who are just taking 3s to take 3s, but for me it set up my game—which really was a mid-range shot. And then getting to the free-throw line."

It still has its detractors. Hall of Fame coach Pat Riley has called it a "gimmick." Longtime *Boston Globe* sportswriter Bob Ryan—whose knowledge of the NBA is rivaled by few—wrote in 2016 that "it's the worst rule development of my lifetime." Even San Antonio Spurs head coach Gregg Popovich said: "I still hate it."

Guess what? This time, it's staying.

O'BANNON V. NCAA

Amateurism Enters a New Court

It had been out there for years: a low-hanging fruit, just begging to be plucked. Ed O'Bannon never really thought about it much, other than the fact that he—like so many people—enjoyed playing video games. But O'Bannon was not just another regular video-game player. Ed O'Bannon was a NCAA championship–winning college basketball player, and a lottery pick in the NBA. The career he, and others, envisioned never came to fruition. But that's not what made O'Bannon unique in this situation; it just played a part. Because almost a decade ago, O'Bannon was playing the EA Sports college basketball video game, *NCAA March Madness*, with a friend when he realized something:

Hey, that's me.

Wait—how did I end up in this game? I didn't give anyone permission.

Then came the most crucial question in all of this: *Why am I not getting paid for this?*

"They literally played me on a video game," O'Bannon told Yahoo! Sports in a 2009 interview. "You could play the '95 Bruins. It didn't have my name, but it had my number, left-handed, it looked like me. It was everything but the name. My friend kind of looked at me and said, 'You know what's sad about this whole thing? You're not getting paid for it.' It was just like, 'Wow, you're right.' It just kind of weighed on me."

That question became the first building block for a lawsuit that would change the discourse about amateur collegiate athletes in this country. Because, if there was money to be made off of the likenesses of college athletes, then why was that money going straight into the pockets of anyone but the athletes? It was a question of fairness, and O'Bannon felt he was being exploited—even long after his collegiate playing days were over. What he did next was akin to throwing a boulder in a small pond.

Former UCLA basketball player Ed O'Bannon in his office.

On July 21, 2009, O'Bannon filed a class-action lawsuit in United States District Court in San Francisco, on what he said at the time was "behalf of all current and former Division 1-A football and men's basketball athletes against the NCAA." The heart of O'Bannon's argument was that he never gave the NCAA the right to use his likeness, during the decade-plus that EA Sports—the producer of both the college basketball and football video games—was putting out the product. With each copy of the video game retailing in the neighborhood of $40 (or more, depending on the console), and both being perennial bestsellers among fans, O'Bannon started doing the math in his head.

It didn't add up.

"When you're in school you're obligated to live up to your scholarship," O'Bannon told Yahoo!. "But once you're done, you physically, as well as your likeness, should leave the university and the NCAA."

The NCAA had always been able to escape any threats against it by players looking to earn money through their status or celebrity in college, citing the legalese in each athlete's scholarship papers. But the video games—and the money being made from them by the schools, in addition to the NCAA's licensing agreements with EA Sports—seemed outside the scope of that authority. How much were some schools taking in from the NCAA's deal with EA Sports? A 2013 ESPN.com article reported that UCLA—O'Bannon's alma mater—received $83,823 from its licensing deal with the video-game maker during the 2012-13 school year.

It's not a massive sum, but it was revenue the school was taking in. And former players like O'Bannon weren't receiving a single cent of it. His lawsuit aimed to change that. Once the

"I want to be clear on a few things: I didn't set out to be the bad guy and we didn't bankrupt college athletics with this suit. We didn't set out to do that. Football Saturdays in the fall are still going to be special, and the tournament in March will still have the madness. As for me personally, I woke up this morning and my bank account is the same. I did not make a dime off this lawsuit. We did this strictly and solely for the betterment of the college athlete."—*Ed O'Bannon, speaking after the 2014 judgment of his lawsuit*

AND ONE!

NCAA failed to get the suit dismissed in 2010, more players began joining O'Bannon's cause: Oscar Robertson and Bill Russell, among them. From there, things began to snowball. As facts and figures on just how much the NCAA, athletic conferences, and colleges were raking in—from lucrative television contracts, to merchandise deals, to licensing agreements—the conversation began to shift.

Enormous sums of money were being dumped into college athletics, primarily in football and men's basketball, with players not reaping any of those benefits—despite being the reasons why the money came in to begin with. In August of 2014, District Judge Claudia Wilken found judgment in favor of O'Bannon that the NCAA's rules were in violation of antitrust law. That ruling lasted just over a year before a three-judge panel for the US Court of Appeals for the Ninth Circuit overturned the decision, throwing out Wilken's decision that the NCAA pay former athletes $5,000 a year in deferred compensation for using their likenesses without permission.

. . . they could wind up with a colossal victory that redefines *amateurism* moving forward.

The matter then headed to the Supreme Court, where as of the summer of 2016, it is still waiting to have its argument heard.

O'Bannon and his fellow plaintiffs may wind up empty-handed, or they could wind up with a colossal victory that redefines *amateurism* moving forward. No matter which side emerges as the winner, any victories or defeats will be parsed over and over. One thing will not be so easily dismissed: the conversation surrounding the topic.

Whether it be through the media or fans in the stands or players finally with the knowledge to speak out about the topic, amateurism in college sports is being discussed. And in more than just a ubiquitous "Pay the players!" or "Don't pay the players!" rant. There are larger issues (and monies) at play that are coming to the forefront. Maybe that wasn't O'Bannon's intention when he filed suit against the NCAA almost a decade ago in a federal court in San Francisco. But it's the legacy—win, lose, or draw—of his decision to do so. And for topics that can easily be overshadowed by wins and losses on the court or on the field, that's a victory that can't be overturned by any court of law.

THE SLAM DUNK

A Signature Basketball Move Arrives—with Authority!

In sports, there exists the rare highlight you know is likely coming, and yet are still surprised to see it when it does happen. In football, it's the touchdown. In baseball, the home run. In hockey, the slapshot goal. For decades, as basketball grew from its infancy as a simple but unrefined game played in the middle of the country to a big-city, ticket-selling commodity, it really had nothing for its fans to hang their hats on. Hard to really get fired up for the Red Auerbach–era Celtics pass-pass-pass-pass-jump shot offense, you know?

Basketball needed a lightning bolt to shock its fans into life. It found one in the slam dunk.

The origins of the first dunk—the big bang's Big Slam, if you will—are a bit muddled. An account in the *Woodland Daily Democrat* has a Barney Dobbas of California-Davis doing a "dunk shot" in 1935. Then there was Joe Fortenberry, a 6'8" Texan, an Olympian, who—in a game at the West Side YMCA in Manhattan—threw one down a year later. There is actual photographic evidence of this one, with a *New York Times* photographer capturing the moment just before Fortenberry is about to put the ball in the basket. There is no mistaking what he is about to do.

And if there was, the legendary *Times* sports columnist Arthur Daley was there to capture it in printed form: "This new version of a lay-up shot, left observers simply flabbergasted.

The Toronto Raptors's Vince Carter sticks his arm through the basket after dunking the ball in the fourth round of the 2000 NBA All-Star Slam Dunk competition.

Joe Fortenberry, 6-foot-8-inch center . . . left the floor, reached up and pitched the ball downward into the hoop, much like a cafeteria customer dunking a roll in coffee."

These men though, were outliers. Basketball was a game played with cunning and one's brain. Phog Allen, one of the game's stewards, wrote in his book *Better Basketball* (published one year after Fortenberry's slam) that "Dunking does not display basketball skill—only height advantage." While that may have been true, Allen and the other founding fathers of the game could never envision someone like Julius Erving taking off from the foul line and throwing it in. Or David Thompson riding an invisible escalator to the hoop. Or Michael Jordan defying gravity. Or Vince Carter dunking over a man who stood 7'2".

The prehistoric dunks were simply quick glimpses into the future.

There is nothing that can electrify a crowd at a basketball game more than a dunk. Three-pointers can certainly bring a crowd to its feet, as can a clutch jump shot, or a nifty layup. But a dunk? When it happens? Everyone in the building feels the energy. A good dunk—a solid *posterization* of the other player—can elicit a visceral reaction. It seems almost insane to imagine a basketball world where someone like LeBron James couldn't take off from the middle of the lane and throw down a dunk with the force of a thunderclap.

But oh, that time existed.

. . . recruits often make mixtapes for YouTube of dunk highlights spliced together.

Dunking, not the powerful type we know today, became common in pro and college basketball in the 40s, 50s, and early 60s. As players like Bill Russell and Wilt Chamberlain entered the sport, dunking became so casual simply because of their height. In 1966, when Lew Alcindor arrived at UCLA, he changed everything. He was so tall and so skilled offensively that he dunked all the time: not as an act of showboating, but because it was so easy. Too easy, the NCAA thought, and it outlawed dunking in college from 1968 through 1977.

"The dunk is one of basketball's great crowd pleasers," Alcindor—now going by Kareem Abdul-Jabbar—wrote. "And there is no good reason to give it up except that this and other n------ were running away with the sport."

He had a point. The majority of the highly skilled offensive players permeating the sport were black. Not allowing dunking limited their games and eventually, their earning potential as showmen in a sport designed for entertainment. Enter the American Basketball Association, which permitted (and encouraged) dunking in games. The upstart league also invented one of the move's greatest showcases: the slam dunk contest.

"It was like, 'Free at last,'" Thompson told the *New York Times* in 2004 about his rookie year playing in the ABA. "The chains were loosened, and I could really show them what I could do. That was real exciting. I hadn't been able to dunk for four years in college, so that first year I tried to dunk every time I could."

Pretty soon, basketball got the memo. The ABA was becoming known as a showcase for these high-flying athletes who could wow a crowd. College basketball lifted its ban on the move soon after. When the NBA merged with the ABA in 1976, it adopted—among other initiatives—the slam dunk contest. All of a sudden, a league that had been plain and boring, was filled with guys like Skywalker (Thompson), Dr. J (Erving), Chocolate Thunder (Darryl Dawkins), The Glide (Clyde Drexler), The Human Highlight Reel (Dominique Wilkins), The Reignman (Shawn Kemp), Air Canada (Carter), and of course, Air Jordan.

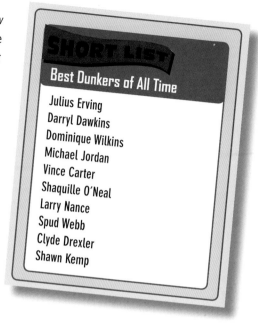

SHORT LIST

Best Dunkers of All Time

Julius Erving
Darryl Dawkins
Dominique Wilkins
Michael Jordan
Vince Carter
Shaquille O'Neal
Larry Nance
Spud Webb
Clyde Drexler
Shawn Kemp

These days, the dunk is still the biggest wow factor at a basketball game, even down to the high school and AAU circuits, where recruits often make mixtapes for YouTube of dunk highlights spliced together. They throw it down, crowd goes wild, rinse and repeat.

"The dunk is so popular because a lot of people who love the game, play the game, watch it as a pastime, can't do those things," Carter told the *Times* in 2004 for a story on the dunk. "You have a chance of doing a behind-the-back pass, a crossover dribble, maybe even hitting a half-court shot. But how many people are going to do a 360 dunk? I think just the amazement of guys being able to get off the ground that high and do things like that is what draws so much attention to the dunk. I can't imagine where my game would be without it."

So the next time you see James or Blake Griffin or Russell Westbrook slam another one home, remember just how far the dunk has come.

GAY PLAYERS

Coming Out to Find a Sport
Accepting of Their Differences

"I'm a 34-year-old NBA center. I'm black. And I'm gay."

Ten words. That's all it took for Jason Collins, a free-agent NBA veteran, to change the way that sports fans viewed someone of a different sexual preference. For years—decades even—hearing the word "gay" in conjunction with the term "professional athlete" seemed like a foreign concept. Our sports heroes were supposed to be the manliest of men: performing astounding feats on the fields of play, drinking some beer afterward, then going home to a super-model woman. Gay players didn't exist in sports in our minds. They couldn't. The locker room, always the bastion of macho culture, couldn't possibly allow it. Couldn't possibly *deal* with it.

There had been players who announced, long after their play-ing days were over, that they were homosexual. Among them were former offensive tackle Kwame Harris, who played six seasons in the NFL (he came out five years after he played his last NFL game), and outfielder Billy Bean, who played six seasons in Major League Baseball (he came out four years after he played his last professional game). There are athletes from golf, tennis, track and field, and elsewhere across the sports landscape who came out—and played—openly, as gay or lesbian.

But an active player? In one of the four major sports leagues in the United States? It seemed like a far-flung, wishful-thinking notion.

Until Collins decided to break the barrier, penning a self-published piece in the May 6, 2013, issue of *Sports Illustrated*, titled "Why NBA Center Jason Collins Is Coming Out Now." At the time the story was released, Collins had completed his 13th NBA season. He was not a superstar, but a serviceable, solid center who had carved out a niche of being a good teammate and a hard worker. But after being traded to Washington midway through

Brooklyn Nets center Jason Collins, after coming out of the closet,
plays against the Los Angeles Lakers on February 23, 2014.

the 2012-13 season and playing sparingly for the team, he felt a stirring inside of him that needed to be made public. He had lived his life in secret, but as he was a free agent, nearing the end of his career, he wanted to be seen for who he really was.

So Collins came out.

"I didn't set out to be the first openly gay athlete playing in a major American team sport," he wrote in *Sports Illustrated*. "But since I am, I'm happy to start the conversation. I wish I wasn't the kid in the classroom raising his hand and saying, 'I'm different.' If I had my way, someone else would have already done this. Nobody has, which is why I'm raising my hand."

Collins was widely praised for his bravery and courage to out himself when he didn't have to. His choice made it easier for others to come forward.

Collins certainly wasn't the first basketball player to come out of the closet. John Amaechi, who played 296 games in the NBA between 1995 and 2003, came out in 2007. Will Sheridan, who was a staple for the Villanova Wildcats, came out in 2011. In the women's game, the acceptance of openly gay players has been a little more widespread. During the 2016 Summer Olympics, four of Team USA's biggest stars—Elena Delle Donne, Brittany Griner, Seimone Augustus, and Angel McCoughtry—were openly gay. Even Rick Welts—a longtime executive in the NBA's offices, and later with the Phoenix Suns and Golden State Warriors—came out in 2011.

"This is one of the last industries where the subject is off limits," Welts said in a 2011 interview with the *New York Times*. "Nobody's comfortable in engaging in a conversation."

These were the first cracks in a dam that burst open when Collins made his announcement. But there was a caveat—he technically wasn't a member of any team. He came out as a free agent. If no one signed him, he'd be just another gay athlete who came out after his

"I know there are more members of the LGBT community who haven't yet stepped forward and (I'm) encouraging them that when they do that the world is ready to accept them and support them. As far as the NBA goes—the NBA is an incredible league. Basketball is a sport of inclusion and diversity and I hope they're able to know how good it will be to be able to live their lives that they want off the court and also be able to have their job on the court." —*Jason Collins*, New York Daily News

AND ONE!

time to make a difference had ended. For a while it seemed that his effort to do so was in vain. He was not invited to any training camp during the 2013 offseason and began the next year without a contract.

Finally, in February, the Brooklyn Nets—the franchise that drafted him—gave him the validation he was looking for: a signed contract. On February 23, 2014, Collins became the first openly gay professional athlete in the four major North American sports leagues to see time in a game. What Collins didn't—or couldn't—know was that his impact had already been felt, just a few hours' drive north.

Players coming out and playing their sport openly—without fanfare, without probing questions—should be the norm . . .

Derrick Gordon, a sophomore starter on the University of Massachusetts men's basketball team, announced in a story with *ESPN* and Outsports.com that he was gay. The news made him the first openly gay player in Division 1 men's basketball. A Plainfield, New Jersey, native who would later transfer to Seton Hall where he would finish his collegiate career, Gordon cited Collins's decision to come out as inspiration.

In March of 2016, when the Pirates made the NCAA Tournament, Gordon became the first openly gay player to play in the event. But in showing just how far the concept of a gay basketball player has come, the milestone was barely acknowledged. Even by Gordon himself.

"I don't have anything to prove to nobody," Gordon said. "The story has been out since 2014, so it shouldn't be a story as it is. My teammates know. Everybody knows."

And shouldn't that be the way it is? Players coming out and playing their sport openly should be the norm, as it should be for any member of society who loves the same sex. In October 2015, Bryant University assistant men's basketball coach Chris Burns announced in *USA Today* that he was gay—the first openly gay coach, of any level in Division 1—men's or women's. The news was a blip on the radar. By the time the season began a few weeks later, Burns was just another coach, grinding out Xs and Os for his team. That spring, San Francisco women's head coach Jennifer Azzi became the first openly gay coach in women's college basketball. She did so while introducing Welts at a Bay Area awards ceremony.

Collins certainly may be viewed as the flag-bearer for players and coaches in the sport of basketball to feel comfortable in coming out. But each bit of news has made it easier for the next one to come out. Meanwhile, the NFL, MLB, and NHL remain places where gay athletes are still a taboo concept. The hope is that the decisions made by Collins and Welts and Sheridan and Amaechi and Gordon and Burns—plus the number of women's basketball players and coaches who have been playing openly for years—can make a dent elsewhere. Because, if nothing else, basketball has proven to be a safe haven.

MAGIC JOHNSON DIAGNOSED WITH HIV

Basketball's Brightest Star Gets a Death Sentence—and Starts a Conversation

Before he could even fully get out the words that he was suddenly retiring, Magic Johnson stood at a podium inside the Great Western Forum in Inglewood, California, and made sure to let everyone know what they were all wondering. He was wearing a dark suit, with a white shirt and muted-colored tie. The three-time Most Valuable Player of the NBA and five-time champion was positioned on a hastily constructed dais, in front of a black-curtained backdrop, with a bevy of distinguished guests on each side. To his right, Hall of Famer Jerry West, Lakers owner Dr. Jerry Buss, team doctor Michael Mellman, and Johnson's wife, Cookie. To his left, NBA commissioner David Stern, friend and former teammate Kareem Abdul-Jabbar, his agent Lon Rosen.

Magic Johnson, arguably one of the most visible people on the planet, had just announced that he was HIV-positive. He quickly followed it up with a caveat that was absolutely necessary:

"I just want to make clear, first of all, that I do not have the AIDS disease. Because I know a lot of you want to know that."

It was something that Johnson had to say that afternoon of November 7, 1991. How could one of the best athletes the country have ever produced announce that he had contracted the HIV virus and not let the world know that he had not yet been diagnosed with AIDS? Johnson had to let his audience—a global one—know that he was not dying. At least he wasn't dying *yet*. More than a quarter of a century later, that seems like a silly thing to have to assert, but on that day in Los Angeles, it was the question on everyone's mind.

Earvin "Magic" Johnson announces his retirement during a
press conference after testing positive for the HIV virus.

How long until Magic Johnson was dead?

It was a question he was asking himself.

"You know, I was like most people: I am going to die," Johnson told the PBS program, *Frontline* in 2011 on the 20th anniversary of his historic announcement. "At the very first (doctor's appointment) when he first announced to me, I thought: 'Oh man, I am going to die. I think it's over.'"

Because in 1991 contracting the HIV virus meant that you were destined to get AIDS. And AIDS was a death sentence. It was a disease that terrified every corner of the globe. It was as

Twenty-five years later, the specter of HIV/AIDS is fading.

mysterious as it was known. There were rumors abound about how it could be contracted: saliva, sneezing, coughing, *holding hands*. Stigmas became attached: It was only a disease confined to the gay community; it was a disease permeated by drug addicts. In reality, it was a disease that seemed absolutely unstoppable. As doctors and scientists raced to find a cure, more and more people were discovered to have the disease.

In 1982, 771 AIDS cases were reported by the Center for Disease Control. The next year, it was 2,807. By 1990, it was a staggering 160,969. Death rates were even scarier: Between 1982 and 1990, the rate of deaths from AIDS-related causes hovered between 75 and 85 percent. So when Johnson announced that he would retire from basketball immediately due to his contraction of the virus that causes AIDS, there was a sense that within five years, he'd be dead. Maybe if he was lucky and stayed in good health and saw the right doctors, he'd make it to his 40th birthday.

"Whatever the reason, how he got it, none of it mattered," Stern told ESPN.com in 2014. "We thought he was going to die. We closed ranks with Magic."

The NBA had to. Johnson had been partly responsible for saving the league over the course of the previous decade. He had made it OK for white fans to root for black players, to see black players as marketable superstars. Before the press conference, as the story leaked out that Johnson was retiring due to the HIV virus, there were cries that he had let the public down, that affairs with women and loose morals were the reason for his plight. There were insinuations that he had contracted the disease from gay sex—a claim Johnson has repeatedly denied. His only explanation: "Sleeping with a lot of women."

The origin of his infection didn't matter. Johnson was now the face of the most feared disease on the planet. He had two choices: hide until his death or be up front, open, and honest about it. Anyone who knew Magic Johnson knew which road he would take. In a conversation with former Lakers trainer Gary Vitti related to ESPN.com 20 years later, Johnson told him: "When God gave me HIV, he gave it to the right person . . . I'm going to do something good with this."

He opened up the national discourse about the disease. The presence of Magic in the conversation made it okay for parents to talk with children about it, teachers to educate about it, and those fearing they might have it to get tested. Johnson meanwhile began taking a drug cocktail designed to keep him alive and stave off the disease. All of it—the education, the conversation, the drugs—worked.

Twenty-five years later, the specter of HIV/AIDS is fading. Johnson, now in his late fifties, has lived with the HIV virus for longer than anyone could have imagined. He is a successful businessman, motivational speaker, and personality. His Magic Johnson Foundation continues to fund and support research to eradicate the virus, but also to get care to those who need it, in addition to testing education. Johnson's success with the mixture of drugs he has been taking has allowed doctors to take similar paths to treat other patients. The CDC estimated that in 2012, nearly 14,000 people in the United States died from AIDS-related causes—which seems high, but is only 8 percent of the total number of deaths in 1991, the year Johnson was diagnosed.

No one should have expected any different from Johnson. After all, he told us so that grim afternoon 25 years ago.

"Life is going to go on for me," he said. "And I'm going to be a happy man. When your back is against the wall, you have to come out swinging. I'm going to go on, going to be there, going to have fun."

"When I first found out I had HIV, I had to find somebody who was living with it, who could help me understand my journey and what I was going to have to deal with day-to-day. I found out a person named Elizabeth Frazier was living with AIDS at the time, and so I called her up and she took a meeting with me. She told me I was going to be here a long time. She told me great drugs were coming down the pipeline. Unfortunately, she was not going to benefit from those drugs."—*Magic Johnson*, Maxim *magazine*

AND ONE!

1965-66 TEXAS WESTERN TEAM

Five Become One Monumental Part of History

Off the court, Texas Western knew what the stakes were. In 1966, when the Miners faced off against the vaunted Kentucky program for the national championship in College Park, Maryland, they trotted out a starting five that was entirely African-American players. Kentucky, meanwhile, was all white. Wildcats head coach Adolph Rupp had five national championships and had been roaming the sidelines in Lexington for over three decades.

He also reportedly once vowed that no black player would ever play at Kentucky.

So when David Lattin—the 6'6" center for Texas Western—threw a dunk down early on in the game over Kentucky's star Pat Riley (yes, *that* Pat Riley), it was a decisive moment. It was clear, from then on: The Miners would be playing for much more than a national championship that March night.

"Adolph Rupp was saying a lot of stuff about us," Harry Flournoy, a forward on that Miners team, told the *Austin American-Statesman* in 2016. "We used that for inspiration. Our mindset was that we were going to win. We had no other thought. We thought we were better than Kentucky." And they were.

Kentucky entered the game at Cole Fieldhouse on the campus of University of Maryland as the No. 1-ranked team in the country—with good reason. The Wildcats were dominant. Despite being one of the smaller teams in the country—they earned the nickname of "Rupp's Runts" because there were no players on the roster taller than 6'5"—Kentucky was

The Texas Western College Miners, 1966 NCAA basketball champions.

SHORT LIST

1965-66 Texas Western Roster

PLAYER	POSITION	YEAR
Jerry Armstrong	Forward	Senior
Orsten Artis	Guard	Senior
Louis Baudoin	Forward	Junior
Willie Cager	Forward	Sophomore
Harry Flournoy	Forward	Senior
Bobby Joe Hill	Guard	Junior
David Lattin	Center	Sophomore
Dick Myers	Forward	Junior
Dave Palacio	Guard	Sophomore
Togo Railey	Guard	Junior
Nevil Shed	Center	Junior
Willie Worsley	Guard	Sophomore

immensely talented. Six players on the roster averaged over 20 minutes a game, giving them an advantage of depth.

Riley (averaging 21.9 points per game)—a forward from Schenectady, New York—had teamed with guard Louie Dampier (averaging 21.1 points per game) from Indianapolis to create a devastating one-two punch. That helped Kentucky roll through its regular season and into the NCAA Tournament with only one loss, to Tennessee on March 5. But as the Wildcats went through the tournament, cracks in the facade started to show.

They beat Dayton in their first game by just seven. The next day, Kentucky edged out Michigan by seven to advance to College Park. Six days later in the national semifinal, Kentucky nipped Duke by four. That set them up against a Texas Western team that seemed to be on a path toward destiny.

The little-known team from El Paso hadn't entered the national conversation until breaking into the Associated Press Top 25 at No. 9 at the beginning of January. The Miners were 23-0 until dropping their only game of the season—coincidentally enough on March 5, as well—to Seattle. They too had needed to eke out two wins in the tournament, beating Cincinnati in overtime and then using two overtimes to beat Kansas and advance to the national semifinals. A seven-point win over Utah brought head coach Don Haskins's team to the brink of a championship.

"I wasn't out to be a pioneer when we played Kentucky," Haskins told the *Los Angeles Times* toward the end of his 38-year career at Texas Western, which became University of Texas at El Paso in 1967. "I was simply playing the best players on the team, and they happened to be black."

Until Haskins rolled out an all-black starting lineup earlier in the year, no college basketball team had started five non-white players in a game—*ever*. He was an old-school coach, not a man on a crusade to break the myth that black players wouldn't be successful without the "guiding hand" of a white player on the floor. He wasn't out to show how Rupp's beliefs and recruiting tactics were out of date and out of touch.

He just wanted to win a basketball game.

Texas Western did, upsetting Kentucky, 72–65, to win the national championship.

"Not in El Paso and not on the road," Haskins wrote in his 2005 autobiography. "Race was just a topic that was brought up by the team. We just played basketball."

Of course, this was America in the fractured 1960s. So people saw the Texas Western win in many ways. The civil rights movement was at its height. Players received hate mail. Haskins, who was white, also was the target of racially charged letters telling him he should have played one of the team's four white players (the Miners also had a Mexican player on their roster) during the game.

. . . the 1965-66 Texas Western win is considered a landmark event in the fight to desegregate sports.

"We were walking around with the medal indicating we were the 1966 NCAA champions," Nevil Shed, one of Texas Western's seven African-American players on that team, recalled to the *Times* in 2008 after Haskins's death. "He was walking around with another brand on him for allowing these players to play. Remember, society wasn't ready for that."

They got it anyway. More than fifty years after that improbable night in College Park, Maryland, the 1965-66 Texas Western win is considered a landmark event in the fight to desegregate sports. A movie inspired by the events surrounding the game, *Glory Road*, was made in 2006. At the 2016 Final Four, the team was honored as part of its 50th anniversary.

Kentucky, by all accounts of those involved in the game, was gracious in defeat. There were no racial slurs thrown, only hands shook. Even Rupp, typically frosty after any loss, greeted the Miners at the end of the handshake line. A reminder that the real racists involved in this monumental game came off the court.

Just like the impact of Texas Western's win.

"When [the] ball goes up on the boards and I go for the rebound, I don't have time to look and see if the other guy is black or white," David Lattin told FoxSports.com in 2016. "I was just going for [the] ball. For our players and for the Kentucky players, there was nothing about race. It was just a lot of young kids that were trying to win."

HARLEM GLOBETROTTERS

Entertaining Popes, Presidents, and People Nightly

On a sleepy morning in May of 2015, Howard Smith—the new president of the Harlem Globetrotters—was in the Sixth Avenue studios of Fox News. He was set to appear on the early-morning program *Mornings With Maria* to talk about some of the new initiatives that he had undertaken since coming aboard a few months earlier. While Smith settled down into his seat on the studio set, off-camera was 5'9" real-life Harlem Globetrotter Tay "Firefly" Fisher, a former college point guard at Siena College in upstate New York, who was dazzling the studio with an array of ball tricks.

Spinning the ball on his finger—a Globetrotter classic—elicited laughs from the usually demure business morning crowd. It was a run-of-the-mill appearance for the Globetrotter organization: laughs, photos, stories, and a parting gift of good feelings.

As soon as Smith and Fisher walked on set, one of the show's panelists, Dagen McDowell, lit up like a Christmas tree. "Oh my gosh, I *loooooooove* the Globetrotters!" she yelped. She immediately began chit-chatting with Smith about the heyday of the team—from the great players, to the constant touring shows, to even the Saturday morning cartoon show. All the while, one of the show's other regulars, Pete Hegseth—himself a former guard for the Princeton Tigers men's basketball team—was snapping selfies with Firefly.

Just another day's work for the team that is undefeated in putting a smile on everyone's face.

"The Globetrotters are an iconic piece of American life," Smith would say later. "They've been around for 90 years, and everyone feels that sense of connection when they come into contact with us."

Wilt Chamberlain, in 1959, wearing the uniform of the Harlem Globetrotters.

On the surface, the Globetrotters may seem a bit cheesy. They're still running some of the same gags that made them famous almost 50 years ago. They don't take themselves too seriously, try to make every fan who attends one of their shows walk away with a memory, and spend over 200 nights on the road a year. They regularly appear on late-night talk shows for skits, help open stock exchanges, and appear all over social media—a platform that seems to have been created just for them.

But that's just part of the Globetrotter story. Before they became one of the most-enjoyed acts in sports or entertainment, the Harlem Globetrotters were pioneers. They broke down racial barriers, and did things that professional sports leagues—aside from the NBA—hadn't

In the 1950s, they made trips to East Germany and communist Russia.

dared to do. They entertained presidents, kings, queens, heads of state, and three popes. When some of the most talented players in college basketball couldn't gain entry into the professional leagues back in the day, they played for the Globetrotters first. Most importantly, during the first 50 years, they existed in a world that saw black and white— and managed to make everyone forget all of that.

The late Meadowlark Lemon—one of the team's most famous members—once said about black fans and white fans attending a Globetrotter game together: "They didn't see color. They saw joy."

"The players of the Harlem Globetrotters were similar to a lot of black men in that generation," then-Senator Barack Obama said in the 2005 documentary, *Harlem Globetrotters: The Team That Changed the World*. "People with enormous talent who couldn't always show their talent, and had to suffer great indignity just to keep food on the table."

What began in 1926 as a promotional gimmick designed to get attention for a new local Chicago nightclub (the team was founded in the Windy City, but had "Harlem" attached to it because the neighborhood was considered the epicenter of progressive black culture in America) turned into something greater. Abe Saperstein, the brains behind the operation, began taking the team barnstorming all over the state of Illinois. Once he saw the crowds that he was drawing, more money was poured into it. At first the Globetrotters weren't an entertainment billing: They were a legitimate basketball team, but after Reece "Goose" Tatum joined the team in 1941, the direction began to shift.

The players worked more comedy routines into games, which quickly began to resemble shows. But the team was profitable, enough to attract top-flight talent. Wilt Chamberlain was a Globetrotter. So were Connie Hawkins and Nat "Sweetwater" Clifton. But the nucleus of the golden era of the Harlem Globetrotters existed during a three-decade run when Marques

Haynes, Meadowlark Lemon, and Curly Neal were staples. They were exquisite showmen, but were also superb basketball players who found a calling outside of the NBA. Chamberlain often said that Lemon was the best player he ever saw. Neal was considered the best dribbler in the sport. Haynes was considered by those in his era to be the best basketball player who never played in the NBA.

After all, you had to have a light-hearted streak to be a Globetrotter, but it wasn't all about being a goofball.

"The comedians were the ones who got cut first," Lemon said in 1977. "You first had to prove that you could play basketball, then you had to show that you could be funny."

It was that constant toeing of the line that made the Globetrotters a hit with everyone. In the 1950s, they made trips to East Germany and communist Russia. They have crossed over to popular culture, starring in movies (1951's *The Harlem Globetrotters*), television (everything from *The White Shadow* to a made-for-TV movie with the cast of *Gilligan's Island* to *The Amazing Race*), and politics (Henry Kissinger, Nelson Mandela, and Jesse Jackson have all been named honorary Globetrotters).

"I grew up in Chattanooga, Tennessee, and my grandparents would take me to see them," actor Samuel L. Jackson said in the documentary. "We had very few opportunities to see African-American athletes, so when the Globetrotters came around, it was a big deal. They were good basketball players and pure entertainers at the same time."

It's been that way for more than 90 years now, with the team kicking off its yearly tour right after Christmas and making stops in every state in the nation, then taking the show overseas. Bringing goodwill, memories, and a bucket full of laughs along the way.

And sometimes a bucket full of water, too.

SHORT LIST

List of Honorary Harlem Globetrotters

Individual	Year
Henry Kissinger	1976
Bob Hope	1977
Kareem Abdul-Jabbar	1989
Whoopi Goldberg	1990
Nelson Mandela	1996
Jackie Joyner-Kersee	1999
Pope John Paul II	2000
Jesse Jackson	2001
Pope Francis	2015
Robin Roberts	2015

KAREEM ABDUL-JABBAR

A Legend by Any Name

The National Basketball Association has had a long lineage of great big men. George Mikan was there at its inception. As the game began to grow, Bill Russell and Wilt Chamberlain carried it along. When the league entered its wild years, Bill Walton and Moses Malone carried the flag. As the league began to take off in popularity, it was Patrick Ewing, David Robinson, and Hakeem Olajuwon who stood tall. As it entered the new millennium, Shaquille O'Neal and Tim Duncan were there. Today there's Anthony Davis and DeAndre Jordan to take the reins.

NO. 15

From the moment it began, the NBA had a marquee big man to point to and say: *He is the best of his generation*.

No one though, can claim to be as good—or as dominant—as one man can: Kareem Abdul-Jabbar.

First off, Abdul-Jabbar has scored more points than anyone in NBA history—38,387. That's almost 1,500 more than Karl Malone, who is the second-highest scorer in league history, and nearly 5,000 more than No. 3, Kobe Bryant. Inevitably someone will think that Michael Jordan is the leading scorer in the annals of the NBA, but they of course would be incorrect—by more than 6,000 points.

Pat Riley, Abdul-Jabbar's former coach, once said: "Why judge anymore? When a man has broken records, won championships, endured tremendous criticism and responsibility, why judge? Let's toast him as the greatest player ever."

But to reduce the greatness of Abdul-Jabbar's legacy to mere points would be a disservice to the man. What sets him apart from all of the other great big men in the history of the NBA is one thing: longevity.

UCLA basketball star, Kareem Abdul-Jabbar,
then known as Lew Alcindor, on March 6, 1967.

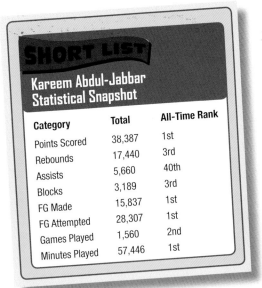

SHORT LIST

Kareem Abdul-Jabbar Statistical Snapshot

Category	Total	All-Time Rank
Points Scored	38,387	1st
Rebounds	17,440	3rd
Assists	5,660	40th
Blocks	3,189	3rd
FG Made	15,837	1st
FG Attempted	28,307	1st
Games Played	1,560	2nd
Minutes Played	57,446	1st

The man who became a national sensation at Power Memorial High School in New York and then a collegiate one at UCLA as Lew Alcindor rode the two unique identifiers of longevity and consistency to success—night in and night out in the NBA. While most great big men in Abdul-Jabbar's era had relatively short careers, he played for 20 seasons and 1,560 games. (Comparatively, Chamberlain played for 15 seasons; Russell for 13; and Walton for 10. Only Shaq approached Kareem's record for longevity, with 19.) Each night for two decades Abdul-Jabbar's team—and conversely, their opponents—knew that he would always be trotting out to midcourt to take the opening tip.

In a 1980 *Sports Illustrated* profile on the star during his fifth season with the Los Angeles Lakers, writer John Papanek recounted a midseason game against the Houston Rockets where Abdul-Jabbar was announced as out with a migraine headache. Sure enough, in the third quarter the Great Western Forum exploded as the Lakers star appeared on the bench. He was immediately inserted into the game, blocked five shots, and made 6-of-7 from the floor—including two Skyhooks over Moses Malone. "I knew it was too good to be true," Rockets coach Del Harris said after the game, which Houston lost. "Bringing in Kareem is like wheeling out nuclear weapons."

And that's perhaps the best way to measure the might of a player who ran the floor like a gazelle, while attacking opponents' shots like a mauling bear, yet was able to gracefully hit a shot as pretty as his Skyhook. A player that good should have some weak point to his game. He shouldn't be allowed to routinely make the lineup card each and every night—the very notion of that seems unfair.

Yet, that was Kareem.

That *Sports Illustrated* story has a litany of quotes given by Adbul-Jabbar's contemporaries about his greatness. (Keep in mind that Abdul-Jabbar would still play for another *nine seasons* after the story was published.)

A sampling:

- Rick Barry, when asked if Kareem was better than Moses Malone: "What kind of ridiculous question is that? Kareem is probably the best athlete in the world."

- Bill Walton: "He's always been my idol. To me, he's the greatest."
- Bob Lanier: "He does things to you that make you ask, 'Damn, now how could a man his size have done something like that?'"
- Jerry West: "A great, great, great basketball player. My goodness, he does more things than anyone who has ever played this game."

He won a championship with the team that drafted him, the Milwaukee Bucks, then changed his name from Lew Alcindor to Kareem Abdul-Jabbar. No matter. He won three Most Valuable Player awards with the Bucks, then after the 1974-75 season, requested a trade to either New York or Los Angeles, to fit his cultural needs. The Lakers sent four players to Milwaukee for Abdul-Jabbar.

Two more MVP awards in his first two seasons in Los Angeles preceded a rebirth of Abdul-Jabbar's career. As most expected him to begin a slow descent after his first decade in the league, the Lakers drafted Magic Johnson and James Worthy—allowing Abdul-Jabbar to be the perfect complementary piece to their "Showtime" offense. Five more titles, another MVP, and countless other accolades later, it was clear that Abdul-Jabbar was the greatest big man—and perhaps player—the game had ever seen.

On March 21, 1990, after Abdul-Jabbar had officially retired, the Lakers retired his No. 33 in a ceremony before their game against the Charlotte Hornets. After congratulatory words from friends, former teammates, coaches, and NBA commissioner David Stern, the microphone was handed over to another former teammate—Magic Johnson. The man who helped spur the run to five titles to close Abdul-Jabbar's career had to catch himself before getting emotional talking about him that night.

. . . it was clear that Abdul-Jabbar was the greatest big man . . . the game had ever seen.

His closing line though, encapsulated everything that anyone would need to know about Kareem Abdul-Jabbar:

"Like Tina Turner said, 'You're simply the best.' And you're definitely better than all the rest."

NCAA TOURNAMENT EXPANDS TO 64 TEAMS

Now the Madness Can Really Begin

NO. **16**

It was formally listed as Proposal No. 91.

That's how the madness began. Slowly, but surely, the NCAA Tournament had been growing since it was first born in 1939. Eight teams, then doubling to 16. Doubling again by 1975. By 1980, it was 48 teams. Four years later, 53 teams were invited, truly making it the "Big Dance." But as college basketball was booming, and as television was getting involved, there was a pocket of the sport that wanted to see more. More teams, more games, more revenue. So in the summer of 1984, it was introduced to the NCAA Executive Committee that the NCAA Tournament should expand to 64 teams for the 1984-85 season.

Proposal No. 91 passed, the field was expanded to 64 teams, and the NCAA truly took over the month of March.

"I think it was just part of the evolution of the basketball tournament," said Sean McManus, chairman of CBS Sports, which has broadcast the event since 1982. "It obviously created more interest because you had double the fan bases that you were appealing to. I think it was one of the most important steps toward making this tournament into what it's become—which is, what I think—in some ways, the biggest and most-followed multi-day sporting event in America."

In 1985 for the first time every team had to play a first-round game. There were no more byes or play-in games for a handful of teams. There would be distinct seeds and regions that would need to be navigated to get to the Final Four. Conference tournament

Valparaiso's head coach Homer Drew hugs his son, Bryce Drew, after Bryce hit a buzzer-beater to beat Mississippi in the 1998 NCAA Tournament.

champions still received automatic bids to the tournament, but expansion meant that teams could play their way into the field much more easily.

Perhaps more than anything, it allowed America to create office pools and gamble on the tournament—because now, it had a full bracket.

"I think it's grown the event," said CBS play-by-play announcer Jim Nantz. "It really gave berth to the Selection Show and that becoming an event of itself. People started getting into the seedings and where are teams going. Before that, it really hadn't caught fire—the whole office pool concept—and now Monday is all about the brackets."

Some have wanted a push toward 96 or 128, but those have been largely quashed.

In 2015, the American Gaming Association estimated that 40 million Americans would fill out more than 70 million brackets ahead of that year's NCAA Tournament. Bigger, they would wager approximately $9 billion on the event—more than double than was bet on that year's Super Bowl ($3.9 billion).

Expanding to 64 teams—and then again to 68 in 2001—has appealed to the country's lust for sports gambling. Even for those with no interest in gambling, the expansion of the tournament provided a reason for non-fans, casual observers, or fans of other teams who didn't make the field to have a rooting interest during the three weeks of the event.

Even former president Barack Obama got into the act, filling out a bracket with ESPN every year he was in office.

"You get people who never watch a college basketball game all year long, suddenly becoming rabid basketball fans because they have the brackets that they've filled out," McManus said. "It's an enormous following for a sport that, during the regular season, doesn't generate the kind of numbers that other sports do."

For a sport that is defined more by the event at the end of its season than what happens in the lead-up to it, expansion of the NCAA Tournament field has allowed college basketball to stay relevant throughout the season. There are now "Bracketologists" who are constantly predicting the postseason fortunes of teams as early as the day after a champion is crowned at the Final Four. Once the sport hits February, fans are constantly following for updated seed projections, where their teams might be headed come tournament time, and if they're on the right or wrong side of the bubble.

"With the expansion, it made a whole lot of sense from a marketing standpoint," said former Duke star Jim Spanarkel, who has called NCAA Tournament games for two decades with CBS. "As you moved from 30 and 40 to 50 and 60, you're just grabbing more people and teams, alums and fans. It allowed for fans to, if their team loses—gravitate to another team and stay interested."

Expansion meant more seeds and manufactured the concept of the "Cinderella story" in the tournament. The seeding concept had only been used for six years prior to expansion in 1985, so when the field was upped to 64, it created chances for major upsets by smaller, unknown teams.

Never was that more apparent than during the 1985 Final Four when a heavily favored Georgetown team was upset by Villanova—a No. 8 seed that year.

"There are incredible stories that you see develop every year," McManus said. "Cinderellas all of a sudden appear. Whether it's a George Mason (in 2006) or a Butler (in 2010), schools—out of nowhere—develop and get huge followings, because of the upset nature of the tournament."

SHORT LIST

15-over-2 Upsets in NCAA History (since 1985)

Year	Winner	Loser	Score
1991	Richmond	Syracuse	73–69
1993	Santa Clara	Arizona	64–61
1997	Coppin State	South Carolina	78–65
2001	Hampton	Iowa State	58–57
2012	Norfolk State	Missouri	86–84
2012	Lehigh	Duke	75–70
2013	Florida Gulf Coast	Georgetown	78–68
2016	Middle Tennessee	Michigan State	90–81

There have been pushes for even further expansion after 2001, when the field grew to 68—adding the "First Four" event, with four play-in games before the tournament begins. Some have wanted a push toward 96 or 128, but those have been largely quashed. There is a point where too much is *too much*. Seeing a 16-seed attempt to knock off a No. 1 loses its luster when the 16-seed comes from a power conference.

"That's why I think it's the best sporting event," Spanarkel said. "The Super Bowl has a natural build-up with playoffs. But there's a sense of urgency on a parallel track, because you have college kids. There's that attachment from the casual fan that you can't get elsewhere." Fans want to see upsets, want to cheer on unlikely stories and players from parts unknown. They want to fill out a bracket, thinking they have correctly identified the dark horses and the sleeper picks. They want the madness, and thanks to Proposal No. 91 being voted in during a meeting in Colorado Springs in the summer of 1984, college basketball gave it to them.

March finally became mad.

RED AUERBACH
Architect of a Dynasty

Start with the cigar.

Chances are if you saw the plume of smoke emanating from the other end of the sidelines, down on the home team bench, you knew what had already happened. You were in the Boston Garden—rickety, old, cramped, smelly—and you were playing the Celtics. Tommy Heinsohn. K. C. Jones. John Havlicek. Sam Jones. Bill Russell. Your work was already cut out for you against the franchise, the building, the players, the history. Gosh, that was almost more than enough.

17

But then for good measure, as you are getting your clock cleaned by the best team in pro basketball and the game is in the closing minutes, you look down the sideline and see the smoke start. And there is Red Auerbach, the Celtics head coach, puffing away at a Hoyo de Monterrey, a sign that he's just wiped the floor with your team.

That was what it was like going up against Auerbach's teams during their great run. It wasn't enough that the Celtics were good and knew they were good, Ol' Red had to light up that trademark victory cigar, sit back, and take it easy.

"Some of the coaches got aggravated," Auerbach told *Sports Illustrated* in 1965. "They thought I was lording it over them. The cigar is a sign of relaxation. The cigarette is a sign of tension. I explained to them that it was an endorsement, that I get money and all the cigars I can smoke. That calmed them down. Why stop a guy from making a buck? However, the fans think this is a major thing."

But during 56 years in Boston, the last thing that Arnold "Red" Auerbach did was blow smoke.

Back in the bad old days of the NBA—when the league played second-fiddle in most of its cities to the college game—the Celtics's franchise was floundering. In its first four years

Auerbach wouldn't be Auerbach without the cigar.

SHORT LIST

Hall of Famers Drafted by Red Auerbach

Player	Year	Round (Pick)
Tom Heinsohn	1956	Territorial
K. C. Jones	1956	2nd (No. 13)
Sam Jones	1957	1st (No. 8)
Satch Sanders	1960	1st (No. 8)
John Havlicek	1962	1st (No. 7)
Jo Jo White	1969	1st (No. 9)
Dave Cowens	1970	1st (No. 4)
Larry Bird	1978	1st (No. 6)
Kevin McHale	1980	1st (No. 3)

of existence, the team never finished above .500. Celtics owner Walter Brown was frustrated by the continued losing seasons. He wanted to not only win, but build a team that would contend year in and year out. Enter Auerbach.

Auerbach had been coaching in the precursor to the NBA—the Basketball Association of America—with the Washington Capitals and Tri-Cities Blackhawks—but was doing far more than most other coaches. He evaluated players and shaped rosters to fit what he felt were the highest needs.

But he wasn't winning either.

Brown had taken notice of what Auerbach had done with the Blackhawks during the 1949-50 season, remaking the roster by trading more than two dozen players. He had found his man.

The Celtics wouldn't finish below .500 for 20 years. Led by Auerbach's tactical strategy on the bench, his keen eye for talent (he drafted or acquired nine future Hall of Famers that he coached) and an unwavering confidence, the Celtics became the model for success in basketball. Between 1957 and 1966, the Celtics made the NBA Finals every single year, winning nine titles—including eight in a row.

"I've seen him laugh, I've seen him cry, I've seen him angry, I've seen him celebrate," Celtics Hall of Famer John Havlicek said after Auerbach's death in 2006. "There's only one guy with the Boston Celtics who has been there for every championship and that is Red Auerbach."

Lighting up those victory stogies after games became only part of the Auerbach legacy.

His ability to rebuild and reload a roster was on full display when he took over full-time as the franchise's general manager following his retirement from coaching. Faced with an aging roster for his hand-picked successor, Bill Russell, Auerbach continued to keep the Celtics dynasty humming. Two more titles in 1968 and 1969. Five straight Atlantic Division titles from 1972 to 1976, with two more championships in 1974 and 1976.

He brought in Dave Cowens, Bailey Howell, and Jo Jo White. Acquired Dave Bing, Pete Maravich, and Bob McAdoo. Pulled off fantastic moves that made people question his judgment . . . until they saw the results.

"It is incredible that [the Celtics dynasty] lasted as long as it did," said former Celtic and current team president of basketball operations Danny Ainge. "And Red was probably the single biggest factor in carrying that forward."

Never was that more apparent than in 1978, when Auerbach used the sixth overall pick in the draft on a player who wouldn't be able to play for them until the following season: Larry Bird. Most talent evaluators didn't know much about Bird since he played for a small school in rural Indiana, but Auerbach did. The ability to shoot, score, and rebound was enough of a reason to make the gamble. (Back then, teams were allowed to retain a player's draft rights for a year.)

He had built and sustained three separate dynasties in Boston . . .

Two years later, Auerbach bolstered another dynasty by shrewdly acquiring Robert Parish in a lopsided trade and then drafting Kevin McHale. The Celtics won five more Eastern Conference championships and three more NBA titles. over the next decade.

He stepped away from the GM's chair in 1984, moving over to dual roles as president and vice chairman. The Celtics never won another championship during his final two decades with the franchise, but he had given it plenty. He had built and sustained three separate dynasties in Boston during his 35 years as coach and general manager. And smoked a lot of victory cigars.

The sight of Red puffing away on another big, fat Cuban meant it had been another good season in Boston. Auerbach's city was captivated. At the original Legal Seafood in Boston, there used to be an item in the fine print at the bottom of the menu. It read:

"No cigar or pipe smoking, except for Red Auerbach."

WILT CHAMBERLAIN
The Legend, the Man, the Myth

Harvey Pollack had the perfect idea. He was pulling quadruple duty that night and needed to create a visual. Pollack was the public relations director for the Philadelphia Warriors on March 2, 1962—but was also asked to cover the game between the Warriors and the New York Knicks in Hershey, Pennsylvania, because the *Philadelphia Inquirer* didn't send the team's beat writer and the Associated Press and United Press International wire services didn't have any reporters who knew much about either team.

NO. 18

So Pollack was drafted into history.

That night, in the Hershey Sports Arena, Wilt Chamberlain—the 7'1" center for Philadelphia—scored 100 points, the most ever scored in a single NBA game. Pollack, serving as the PR man *and* reporter, knew that the Associated Press photographer, Paul Vathis, would need some sort of visual to play for the next day's papers. After a couple of minutes, Pollack had it: He scribbled "100" on a piece of white paper and handed it to Chamberlain to hold.

There, in the cramped, dank locker room—with suit jackets and pants hanging around him—is the man who orchestrated the greatest single-game performance in the history of the sport, marking it on a single piece of paper.

"As time goes by, I feel more and more a part of that 100-point game," Chamberlain told NBA.com, more than 30 years after the feat. "It has become my handle, and I've come to realize just what I did."

Wilt Chamberlain of the Philadelphia Warriors holds a sign reading "100"
after he scored 100 points against the New York Knickerbockers.

In some ways, Chamberlain's legacy—tied to a single game and a single piece of crude visual evidence—is the perfect touchpoint for his career and life. Wilt Chamberlain's entire basketball existence is defined by numbers.

Most points in a game? Wilt. (100.) Most points in a half? Wilt. (59.) Most field goals in a game? Wilt. (36.) Most rebounds in a game? Wilt. (55, November 24, 1960 vs. Boston.) Most minutes in a season? Wilt. (3,882 in 1961-62.) Highest points-per-game average in a season? Wilt. (50.3 in 1961-62.) Most points in a season? Wilt. (4,029 in 1961-62.) Most 50-point games? Wilt. (45 in 1961-62.) Highest field-goal percentage? Wilt. (72.7 percent in 1972-73.) Most free throws attempted? Wilt. (1,363 in 1961-62.) Highest rebounds-per-game average? Wilt. (27.2 in 1960-61.)

> **. . . Chamberlain's career was—rightly or wrongly—defined by the night he scored 100 points.**

And please, if you thought Wilt's statistical exploits were confined to just one season or one short burst in a 14-year career, think again.

Most minutes per game over a career? Wilt has that, too. (45.8 over 14 seasons.) Most games of 60 or more points? Why, that's Wilt, of course. (32.) How about most games of 50 or more points? Better believe it's Wilt. (118!) Most consecutive games of 50-plus points? Wilt again. (Seven from December 16 to 29, 1961.) Most seasons leading the league in free throw attempts? Yes, it's Wilt. (Nine—including six straight from 1959-60 to 1964-65.) Most rebounds? Who else, but Wilt. (23,924—2,304 more than the No. 2 on the list, Bill Russell and *6,484 more* than No. 3, Kareem Abdul-Jabbar.)

There is arguably no player in the history of professional basketball who has his fingerprints on more records than Wilton Norman Chamberlain.

"Open up the record book and it will be obvious who the greatest is," Larry Bird once told a reporter, when asked who the greatest player of all time is.

And really, there wasn't a piece of basketball history that Chamberlain didn't touch.

Born in the Overbrook section of Philadelphia, Chamberlain was a frail child who didn't initially have any interest in the sport of basketball. He enjoyed track and field, but as he matured, his body frame grew to proportions that few had seen. By the time he was a freshman at Overbrook High School in 1951, Chamberlain was a freakish 6'11". He was an immediate standout on the basketball court, where he was still learning to love the game.

Following Chamberlain's death in 1999, Associated Press sportswriter Hal Bock wrote of "The Big Dipper": "Wilt Chamberlain was scary, flat-out frightening. That's because before he came along most basketball players were mortal-sized men. Chamberlain changed all that."

It was true. By the time he was a senior, Chamberlain amassed over 200 recruiting offers from nearly every school in the country. Kansas, and legendary head coach Phog Allen, eventually won the recruiting prize of the century. In Lawrence, Chamberlain was a two-time All-American and won the Most Outstanding Player award in the 1957 championship—despite the Jayhawks' triple-overtime loss to North Carolina, with a 23-point, 14-rebound performance.

Chamberlain would leave Kansas before his senior year, joining the Harlem Globetrotters before making his NBA debut in 1959. It was a career dripping with accolades and success. He won two NBA championships (albeit, later in his career with the Philadelphia 76ers and Los Angeles Lakers), four MVP awards, and was a 13-time All-Star. (There was also the self-proclamation in his 1991 autobiography that he had slept with nearly 20,000 women in his lifetime.)

"Wilt was one of the greatest ever," said Kareem Abdul-Jabbar, a former teammate and friend after Chamberlain's death. "We will never see another one like him."

More than anything though, Chamberlain's career was—rightly or wrongly—defined by the night he scored 100 points.

"I get constant reminders from fans who equate that game and my career as one and the same," Chamberlain said of his 100-point night years after. "People don't talk about the 50-point average, the 69-13 Lakers championship team I played for. They talk about the night I scored 100. That's my tag, whether I like it or not."

On the Legacy of Wilt Chamberlain

"He was more inquisitive than anybody I ever knew. He was writing a screenplay about his life. He was interested in world affairs, sometimes he'd call me up late at night and discuss philosophy. I think he'll be remembered as a great man. He happened to make a living playing basketball, but he was more than that. He could talk on any subject. He was a Goliath."—*Sy Goldberg, Chamberlain's longtime attorney, in 1999*

AND ONE!

LeBRON JAMES
The Newest King Ascends to the Throne

The story idea was a simple one. It was 2002, and there was a high school junior who was quickly becoming the newest product of the high school basketball summer circuit hype machine. The previous summer, at the ABCD Camp in New Jersey—a cattle call for the best and brightest high school prospects in the country—he had effectively gone one-on-one against Lenny Cooke, then considered the top high school player. This kid had dusted Cooke. Suddenly, *he* was the "it" player.

NO. 19

As he began to play his penultimate high school season, word began to slip out: He was not only good, he was pro-ready good. He would not be playing in college. He was already hearing pitches from sneaker companies. Sneaker companies, in turn, were looking to him to follow in the lineage of Michael Jordan and Kobe Bryant.

All of this seemed to be incredibly rarified air to Grant Wahl, then a national college basketball writer for *Sports Illustrated*, who pitched a story to his editors about this kid. *Go out and profile him*, he was told.

"It was kind of quaint, the whole thing," Wahl remembered. "He was a kind, respectful kid. We watched Damon Wayans videos in the apartment he shared with his mom. He had a binder of his favorite CDs that he showed me. But when we went out, you could see just how big he had gotten."

It was in that 2,148-word cover story that the world was first introduced to LeBron James of Akron, Ohio. Not the one-man basketball superpower he would later become. Not the heir apparent to the throne of Jordan. Not the man who broke his hometown's heart and then was welcomed back—and then won it back forever, leading the Cavaliers to the championship in 2016. When James first graced the cover of the magazine in Wahl's story,

LeBron James during his first stint with the Cleveland Cavaliers in 2009.

he was a teenager having fun, loving basketball, and earning the praise of almost everyone who saw him play.

He was raw and uncut, not the molded and scripted version that would emerge nearly a decade later. James was an unfiltered portrait of the future greatness that put him in the same breath as the greatest players ever to pick up a basketball.

"As far as this game, it's just a joy to watch him," Hubie Brown, former head coach and current television analyst, told ESPN.com in 2015. "Because not only is the athleticism at the highest quality ever, but his basketball IQ on top of all that is as good as anybody who has ever played the game."

From the very beginning of James's explosion onto the basketball stage, it was apparent that he was destined for great heights. Even as a skinny teenager first dominating for St. Vincent-St. Mary High School, James seemed to defy logic. How could a player with a 6'8" frame run the floor like he could? Have the court vision that he had? Do the things that he was able to do? Leaping in the air for dunks seemed effortless. His massive hands made the ball look like a piece of fruit in his palms. After he was drafted by his hometown Cleveland Cavaliers straight out of high school in 2003, he immediately bulked up to 250 pounds. He was the rare player who could play multiple positions, both well and effectively.

Upon viewing James for the first time in 2001 as a high schooler, longtime *Sporting News* writer Mike DeCourcy wrote the following about the future marvel: "All that you've heard about his ability is true, except that it may be incomplete. The first thing that came to mind upon watching him was this: Magic Johnson's head on Michael Jordan's body."

"They said u lost a step, wasn't explosive as once was, the best days was in the real view, questioned your drive, your leadership, your commitment, you don't have killer instinct, going back home is the worst mistake in your career, he got the coach fired, players traded, won't work between him and Kyrie, Him and Kev won't work, love your teammates to much, there's no way he can deliver a championship in his hometown, etc etc etc. . . . But guess what THATS NONE OF MY BUSINESS"—*LeBron James on Instagram after bringing a championship to Cleveland*

AND ONE!

Most Valuable Player awards soon followed. (Four of them, in fact.) All-Star appearances and first-team all-league recognitions were sure bets. In time, the championships would also come—though for those who will always (and constantly) measure James's career against that of Jordan's, it seems to never be enough. Much like the other transformative NBA stars, James has seamlessly transitioned to movies and TV, music and business. Yes, he took four years of grief for his handling of free agency in 2010, when he bolted the Cavaliers for the Miami Heat— setting up shop with two other superstars in a transparent grab for rings. That misstep though, was absolved when James showed how much brighter his star was when he was finally surrounded with other ones.

From the first moment we met LeBron James, we knew of his destined greatness.

In short, he is the latest torchbearer for the NBA and the game of basketball.

With that though, comes the responsibility of always having to be measured against the greatest players to ever play. He's still in his early 30s, which means there's plenty of time left in his career. He can win more championships. He can score more points, or set more records.

But it is clear James is a player with unmatched physical skills. That alone puts him on the pedestal alongside the Chamberlains, the Abdul-Jabbars, the Johnsons, the Birds, and the Jordans of the sport.

"When I see LeBron James, I see the best and most dominant player in the game," former teammate Dwyane Wade once told reporters.

Which is why that first glimpse into James and his life back in *Sports Illustrated* 15 years ago is almost like a time capsule. From the first moment we met LeBron James, we knew of his destined greatness. There are no magazine profiles about a teenage Michael Jordan or a teenage Magic Johnson. Their legends were constructed long after their spectacular play made them noteworthy.

The 2,000-plus words on James and the growing legend serve as a reminder that the hype was real. That yes, he was supposed to and *did* become that good. That when we thought he might become one of the all-time greats, we were correct.

"You have a feeling when your timing is right," Wahl remembered of his first encounter with James. "When you're catching something special at just the right time, it's a pretty cool feeling. It doesn't come around all that often. That's what I felt about being around LeBron then."

Wally Johansen · Slim Wintermute · Bob Anet · Howard Hobson · Laddie Gale · John Dick

Bob Hardy · Carl M. Neely · Jay Langston · Ford Mullen · Matt Pavalunas · Bob officer · Ted Sarpola · Earl Sandness

CREATION OF THE NCAA TOURNAMENT

A March Ritual Is Born

Harold "Oley" Olsen wasn't the kind of man who you said no to easily.

By the start of the 1938-39 season, Olsen had been the head basketball coach at Ohio State for 16 seasons. His teams were always solid, competitive squads, but still stuck in the middle of the always strong Big Ten Conference. He had two first-place finishes under his belt—in 1924-25 and 1932-33—but that was it. Still, he was a major figure in the Buckeye athletic department and had influence nationally, having served as the past president of the National Association of Basketball Coaches.

Like every one of his compatriots, he took notice when the Metropolitan Basketball Writers Association started the National Invitation Tournament (NIT). Beginning with the 1937-38 season, the organization held its postseason tournament under a single, simple premise: to determine a national champion.

It invited six teams to play in a single-elimination tournament, with the championship game being played at Madison Square Garden in New York City.

Until then, college basketball was primarily a regionalized sport. Teams from local areas played only nearby teams; or if a school was part of a conference, its primary competition was from teams within its own league. But the MBWA—in particular, Ned Irish, who had covered the sport for the *New York Telegram* until the mid-1930s—believed that college basketball needed to be given a national showcase with which to shine.

The 1938-39 University of Oregon basketball team—NCAA Champions.

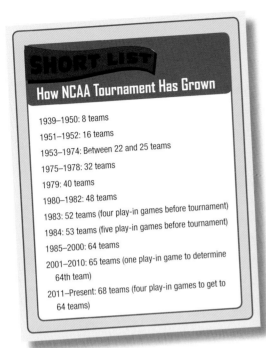

SHORT LIST

How NCAA Tournament Has Grown

1939–1950: 8 teams

1951–1952: 16 teams

1953–1974: Between 22 and 25 teams

1975–1978: 32 teams

1979: 40 teams

1980–1982: 48 teams

1983: 52 teams (four play-in games before tournament)

1984: 53 teams (five play-in games before tournament)

1985–2000: 64 teams

2001–2010: 65 teams (one play-in game to determine 64th team)

2011–Present: 68 teams (four play-in games to get to 64 teams)

At the conclusion of the 1937-38 season, six teams were chosen: Oklahoma A&M (now Oklahoma State), Colorado, Temple, Bradley, New York University, and Long Island. Temple would beat Colorado in the final to win what was considered the first true national championship. (Though, two years earlier, the Helms Foundation in Los Angeles had begun awarding "national championships" in basketball and football, but their system wasn't rooted in a tournament.)

Either way, Temple was crowned the national champions. By a group of New York sportswriters.

Harold Olsen thought college basketball could do better.

He knew there were teams that should have been invited to participate in the NIT that first season that were conspicuously left out. Olsen felt the writers wanted to sell tickets—make the event a big spectacle so they would have something grand to write about. After all, Irish had done such a good job of efficiently organizing big-ticket games that he quit the *Telegram* in 1935 to begin organizing and promoting college basketball games for Madison Square Garden. Schools that could afford to take their teams to New York City to play in these marquee games for a small profit—but gain national exposure—flocked to Irish.

Olsen thought the fix had been in against teams from the midwestern and western parts of the country, and that there needed to exist a tournament representative of the entire collegiate landscape from coast to coast.

His solution? Create a rival tournament.

There was one difference: With the backing of the NABC and the National Collegiate Athletic Association, this new tournament would truly be able to lay claim to crowning the national champion for college basketball. Not a group of cigar-smoking, whiskey-drinking, gambling-on-the-side sportswriters.

"The prestige of college basketball should be supported and demonstrated to the nation by the college themselves," Olsen once wrote in *Ohio State Monthly*. "Rather than be left to private promotion and enterprise."

It was a convincing argument by the Ohio State head coach. The NCAA liked the idea of creating a tournament that could properly—and fairly—identify a national champion. To guard against any favoritism or regionalism, Olsen added another wrinkle to his idea: a selection process divvied up throughout the country. There would be four teams from the eastern half of the country, and four teams from the western half of the country.

Eight teams in all, chosen by the committee—led by Olsen— who would play single-elimination until a champion was crowned. The championship game would appropriately enough be held in the middle of the country, at Patten Gymnasium on the campus of Northwestern University.

. . . the NIT still held sway until the 1950s, when the NCAA mandated that if a team won its conference, it had to play in the NCAA Tournament . . .

Olsen's idea was an instant hit. Probably even more so on his own campus, as Ohio State won the Big Ten title and was one of the eight teams selected into the tournament field. The Buckeyes then knocked off Wake Forest in the quarterfinals, trounced Villanova in the semifinals, before falling by 13 to Oregon in the championship game. Nevertheless, Olsen went on to coach Ohio State for seven more seasons, before leaving to take the head job with the Chicago Stags of the newly formed Basketball Association of America, which would become the NBA.

Even though the NCAA Tournament had to initially grapple with the NIT over prestige— the NIT still held sway until the 1950s, when the NCAA mandated that if a team won its conference, it had to play in the NCAA Tournament—it eventually overtook and surpassed its predecessor. Both tournaments still exist, but the NCAA Tournament is far and away the bigger of the two. The NIT (owned and operated by the NCAA since 2005) is viewed as the second-tier event for teams that don't make the NCAA field.

As for that other tournament? Well, between Selection Sunday, year-round Bracketology, Who's In, Who's Out, 68 teams, Sweet 16s, Elite Eights, Final Fours and "One Shining Moment"—it's pretty clear that Harold Olsen was certainly on to something.

THE NBA LOGO
An Iconic Symbol Born out of Simplicity

The NBA had a problem.

For 20 years, the league had been the only game in town. Professional basketball had finally started thriving in the 1950s, after the Minneapolis Lakers dynasty was born. The 1960s boom was led by the Boston Celtics's winning ways being beamed into every television set in the country. But in 1967, the American Basketball Association was born. A league that played with a flair and style all its own, it was distinctly different from its bigger, more established brother.

NO. 21

The ABA was in new markets—New Jersey and New Orleans, Denver and Indianapolis—with characters who were larger than life. Players who weren't eligible for the NBA draft were immediately able to hone their talents in the ABA. (The NBA stuck to its rule of not allowing players to enter the league who had not completed the collegiate eligibility.) The pace of play was faster, more offensive-minded. There was the institution of the 3-point line and a 30-second shot clock. It was everything the NBA wasn't. And the league began to get worried.

It had no television partner until ABC came aboard in 1964. Attendance league-wide was stagnant. There were only 14 teams, but only a handful could claim profitability. In short: The NBA had an identity crisis. J. Walter Kennedy, the league's commissioner, sensed the need for the league to brand itself, to stand out from its emerging competitor and firmly establish that *it*, not the ABA, was the place to watch the best competitive professional basketball.

Kennedy decided the league needed a logo.

The National Football League introduced its "shield" logo in 1960, giving it an iconic, distinct identity. The National Hockey League had had an official league logo for almost 50

A detail showing the NBA logo on the New York Knicks new away game uniform on September 6, 2012.

years. But Major League Baseball—the oldest professional sports league in North America—hadn't had a logo until the 1969 season.

Baseball's logo of a batter's silhouette was originally intended to be used as a patch to signify the league's 100th anniversary season in 1969. But it was so popular that the league adopted it for good. Kennedy saw what the marketing firm of Sandgren & Murtha had done for Major League Baseball and decided that was what he wanted for his league. The NBA needed a logo, so he went shopping for an agency, landing with Manhattan-based Siegel+Gale.

Kennedy tasked the young firm to create something that would identify the NBA as the "national league of basketball," similar to what MLB had done with its logo—something simple and easy to market, yet unique and easily identifiable. Co-founder Alan Siegel immediately set out to accomplish the task.

He began sketching out ideas and different designs, but none of them worked. Having worked at Sandgren & Murtha alongside the creator of the MLB logo—Jerry Dior—he wanted to echo baseball's design. The use of red, white, and blue to link it with the country. The clean lines, making it easily noticed. Something that worked on a piece of paper as well as it did on a T-shirt or hat. There was always a rumor that Dior had based the MLB logo on the batting stance of Minnesota Twins star Harmon Killebrew. (It wasn't true.)

That gave Siegel an idea: Model the logo after a player.

He wanted a player that would fit what the league stood for. It couldn't be a player trying to dunk, because that felt too ABA. It couldn't be a player shooting a jump shot, because the image would be too clunky. He asked his close friend, Dick Schaap—the legendary sportswriter and then-editor of *Sport* magazine—if he could have access to their photo archive. Schaap, who had known Siegel since they were kids, said of course. So Siegel pored through

On First Seeing the Photo of Jerry West That Became the Logo

"I found this picture of Jerry West dribbling down the court, and of course, growing up in New York and my father having season tickets for college and pro games at Madison Square Garden, I'd see West play a lot."— *Alan Siegel*, Los Angeles Times

AND ONE!

photos until he came upon the perfect one: a photograph by Wen Roberts of Los Angeles Lakers star Jerry West driving to the hoop with the ball in his left hand.

"It had a nice flavor to it," Siegel told the Los Angeles *Times* in a 2010 interview. "So I took that picture and we traced it. It was perfect. It was vertical and it had a sense of movement. It was just one of those things that clicked."

Kennedy agreed, and the logo was born.

. . . the logo generates over $3 billion a year in licensing for the league.

The NBA has always played coy over the years, continually declining to say if the image was actually based on West's likeness or not. Siegel has said that it was, and his firm's website—which still lists the NBA logo as a case study for prospective clients—acknowledges that the West photo birthed the logo.

"They want to institutionalize it rather than individualize it," Siegel told the *Times*. "It's become such a ubiquitous, classic symbol and focal point of their identity and their licensing program, that they don't necessarily want to identify it with one player."

It hardly would matter if they did. The NBA logo, finished by Siegel in 1969, officially debuted in time for the 1971-72 season—the league's 25th anniversary (the only time West would win a NBA title). Since then, it's become one of the most recognized logos in all of sports. Nearly 50 years after its initial creation, the logo generates over $3 billion a year in licensing for the league.

And most importantly, cemented the NBA—not the ABA—as the premier professional basketball league.

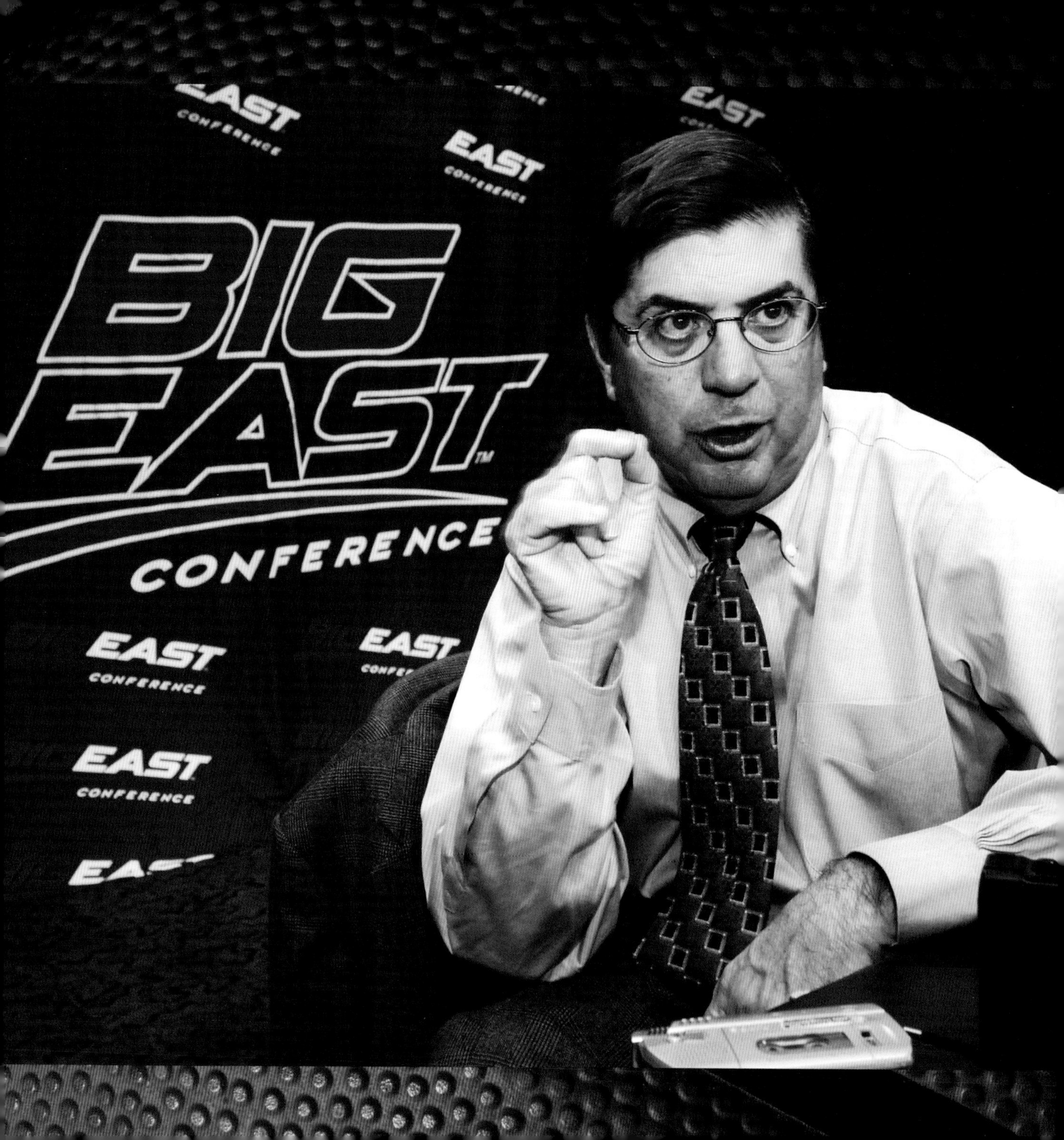
BIG EAST
CONFERENCE
EAST
CONFERENCE

THE BIG EAST CONFERENCE

The Biggest, Baddest College Basketball League Ever Created

"We're going to play at Madison Square Garden."

At this point, Dave Gavitt finally had everyone in the room, so he figured, why not go for broke? The former head coach and now athletic director at Providence College had pulled every string, called in every favor, schmoozed every last straggler to get this deal done. Gavitt had convinced seven schools—anchored by basketball and not football—to form a new league where their sport would be front and center.

On May 31, 1979, the Big East Conference was officially born.

In typical Gavitt fashion, he didn't stop there. He knew that his new league would be anchored by teams with major media markets. There needed to be an annual event to put the new conference on display. So after the handshakes were made and with the ink barely drying on the contracts, Gavitt announced the centerpiece to his plan: a conference tournament in New York City, to begin no later than the fourth year of Big East play.

"We never thought we'd get to New York in Year 4," Tom McElroy, the league's former public relations director at the time, recalled. "I think the master plan was getting there in Year 8 if this thing took hold."

Now, to understand how this far-flung, crazy plan came to fruition, you have to understand the force of nature that was Dave Gavitt. At the time the conference was created, college basketball was still a regionalized sport, in the East in particular, where the Eastern

Former Big East commissioner Mike Tranghese talks to reporters in 2005 during Big East NCAA college basketball media day at Madison Square Garden in New York.

SHORT LIST

NCAA Men's Basketball Champions from the Big East Conference

Year	Champion
1983–84	Georgetown
1984–85	Villanova
1998–99	Connecticut
2002–03	Syracuse
2003–04	Connecticut
2010–11	Connecticut

Collegiate Athletic Conference was the homogenized home for dozens of top-flight teams. Problem was, the NCAA Tournament was always won by teams that faced stiff competition night in and night out. They played their games on TV, giving them a recruiting advantage, and kept the machine rolling year after year.

Gavitt thought that basketball in the Northeast—an area of the country that had not produced a champion since La Salle in 1954—was too ripe of an entity to not be a major player. So he recruited Syracuse, got a fellow Friar, John Thompson, to convince Georgetown to join, drank wine with Lou Carnesecca of St. John's on a trip to Italy to sway him, and added Boston College, Connecticut, and Seton Hall. All of them would join his Providence program as founding members. A year later, Villanova was added.

Suddenly, even the skeptics in his own house—and there were plenty—started to see the vision.

"We were so fortunate in so many ways at the outset," Gavitt said in a 2006 interview. "We put together a solid foundation with a good plan, but we were fortunate to have four coaches who were going to be at their schools for a long time in John Thompson, Louie Carnesecca, Jimmy Boeheim, and Rollie Massimino."

As the league partnered with a burgeoning sports network—ESPN—for its TV package, the Big East took off. Pretty soon, as the landmark 1981 recruiting class (Patrick Ewing at Georgetown, Chris Mullin at St. John's, and Ed Pinckney at Villanova) arrived in the league, it had the push it needed to go to Madison Square Garden.

From there, the league exploded into the stratosphere.

Between 1982 and 1989, the Big East had a team in the Final Four eight times. (Only Boston College, Connecticut, and newly added Pittsburgh failed to make it.) In 1985, three of the four teams were conference members. It won national championships in 1984 (Georgetown) and 1985 (Villanova)—plus had members lose in the final possessions in 1982 (Georgetown), 1987 (Syracuse), and 1989 (Seton Hall).

"These downtrodden programs were turning into powerhouses overnight," said John Paquette, who has been the league's communications director since 1990, after moving over from Seton Hall. "They were using the TV deal to do it. The sales pitch was easy: 'Help us get better, build the program and you'll be on TV all the time.'"

Soon enough, the Big East was the envy of college basketball. But with success, came pitfalls. The league had to expand to satisfy the members who had football teams to schedule, adding four more teams by 1995. Gavitt had left to join the front office of the Boston Celtics in 1990, leaving the reins to his right-hand man, Mike Tranghese. But even the steady hand of Tranghese—who was the league's first full-time employee—couldn't save it from the path it was headed down.

Miami, Virginia Tech, and Boston College bolted for the riches of the Atlantic Coast Conference in 2004 and 2005. To compensate for the losses, the Big East added more freight: Cincinnati, Louisville, and South Florida for football and basketball; DePaul and Marquette for basketball. While the league continued to be a behemoth on the basketball side, football continued to be the wedge that drove the league apart.

The final blow came on September 17, 2011, when late on a Friday night, founding member Syracuse and longtime member Pittsburgh announced they were leaving . . .

"Everything started moving everywhere," Paquette recalled. "And we were always the league with 'some basketballs' and 'some footballs' and that probably made us vulnerable."

The final blow came on September 17, 2011, when late on a Friday night, founding member Syracuse and longtime member Pittsburgh announced they were leaving the conference to join the ACC. West Virginia would soon leave for the Big 12 and Rutgers for the Big Ten; Louisville would also join the ACC later.

"It's kind of like when you lose your job and you get a new job—you better be excited about it," Boeheim said during his final Big East tournament in 2013. "You don't have your old job anymore. You take the hand you're dealt."

A couple of hours after the news of Syracuse and Pittsburgh's departure, Dave Gavitt died at the age of 73. The cause was congestive heart failure.

His dream, though, died of a broken heart.

THE FINAL FOUR

College Basketball Coins Its Big Event

Two words.

That's really it. We use them so often and so effortlessly now that it seems inconceivable that once they didn't exist in the way we think of them today. Two words that are thrown around so often that they get linked to almost everything.

Have a bunch of presidential candidates? The race doesn't start until there's a final four.

Trying to pick from a bunch of restaurant options for dinner? *Give me your final four.*

Come to conference championship weekend in the NFL? *It's the final four.*

The *Final Four*. Two words that when finally placed together by a Cleveland sportswriter in 1975 as part of a freelance article for a now-defunct college basketball preview magazine would change the way the sport's biggest event is viewed. From the time the first NCAA Tournament was played in 1939 all the way until 1977, the concluding weekend was simply referred to as what it was: the national semifinals.

No glitz. No glam. No days of hype by networks. That all changed in 1978.

"It's an incredibly appealing name," said Sean McManus, chairman of CBS Sports, which has broadcast the tournament and Final Four since 1982. "It has caught on so much that people now apply it to other sports. It's become part of the sporting public's vernacular."

So much so that it seems impossible to separate "Final Four" and "college basketball." The two terms are now so intertwined, having been linked together in 1978. That was three

Villanova's Kris Jenkins shoots the game winning three-point basket in the 2016 NCAA Final Four.

years after the NCAA officials in Indianapolis had caught wind of a throwaway paragraph in a story in the *1975 Official Collegiate Basketball Guide*. Inside the green and white-lettered cover with UCLA's star forward Dave Meyers on the cover, Ed Chay had written a story recapping the 1974-75 season.

Ticket prices have skyrocketed as the Final Four becomes a bucket-list destination for every sports fan.

Chay, a longtime sportswriter at the *Cleveland Plain Dealer*, was a staple covering college football and basketball. He covered Ohio State for more than 20 years for the paper, but also contributed stories to the annual preseason magazine. On page 5 of the 1975 edition, Chay wrote the following about Marquette, which had lost in the championship game the year prior to North Carolina State:

"Outspoken Al McGuire of Marquette, whose team was one of the final four in Greensboro, was among several coaches who said it was good for college basketball that UCLA was finally beaten."

There it was for the first time associated with college basketball: the words "final four."

It made perfect sense. Starting in 1952, the final four teams always made it to the final destination at the end of the event. But it wasn't until Chay called it a "final four"—lowercase, mind you—that it dawned on anyone to call it that. Even the NCAA, which took three more years to finally decide to use the term "Final Four" in labeling its 1978 version, was slow to pick it up.

Now, the Final Four—capitalized—is big business. College basketball's premier event is on par with the Super Bowl and national championship game for college football as one of the biggest sports events in the country. It's moved out of the courts of smaller, mid-sized arenas and is strictly held in massive stadiums now. It draws crowds of more than 70,000 people, has elevated courts, and hundreds of media members each year.

The NCAA has trademarked the term, and if you think that's a joke, just ask Coors Brewing Company, which was sued by the organization in 2002 for an unapproved promotion using "Final Four."

Plus, it was free to acquire. Chay never thought of his innocuous line in the story as a potential money-maker for himself or anyone else. To him, it was just a natural iteration to call the four teams at the end of the tournament, "the final four." That wasn't the case for the NCAA when it tried to use two phrases now commonly associated with the tournament. The NCAA had to pay $50,000 in the mid-1990s to the Kentucky High School Athletic Association to use "Sweet 16" after the KHSAA registered its trademark in 1988, after over 70 years of use.

A few years before that settlement, the NCAA and the Illinois High School Association both claimed to own the rights to "March Madness," but the IHSA actually had used it first in a 1939 self-published magazine. The legal back-and-forth finally resulted in a compromise: the establishment of the March Madness Athletic Association, a joint holding company, where the IHSA controls the name on the high school level, while the NCAA has a perpetual license to use the phrase at the college level.

None of that happened with the phrase "Final Four." Chay continued his career as a sportswriter, before dying in Florida in 1997. The NCAA had been using his Final Four term for two decades at that point. (It is not known if Chay ever received any retroactive royalties for coining the term.) The year after they first decided to use Final Four, the NCAA tournament struck gold, with a national semifinals and championship game for the ages—Michigan State versus Indiana State—featuring two future legends: Magic Johnson and Larry Bird. It's still the most-watched NCAA championship game in history.

SHORT LIST

Top Five Most-Attended Final Fours (through 2016)

Year	Site	Attendance	Teams
2014	Irving, TX	79,444	UConn, Kentucky, Florida, Wisconsin
2016	Houston, TX	75,505	Villanova, North Carolina, Syracuse, Oklahoma
2011	Houston, TX	75,421	UConn, Butler, Kentucky, VCU
2013	Atlanta, GA	75,350	Louisville, Michigan, Wichita State, Syracuse
2012	New Orleans, LA	73,361	Kentucky, Kansas, Ohio State, Louisville

The hype has built for the event every year since. Television contracts to broadcast the Final Four have brought the NCAA incredible amounts of revenue. Media attention continues to grow. Ticket prices have skyrocketed as the Final Four becomes a bucket-list destination for every sports fan.

In 2017, the Final Four will travel to Glendale, Arizona—outside of Phoenix—for the first time. With the ability to approach 80,000 fans, the University of Phoenix Stadium will make a run at breaking the all-time attendance mark set in 2014.

Hard to imagine that for something called "National Semifinal weekend."

Thanks to Ed Chay, we don't have to.

PAT SUMMITT

A Benchmark for Greatness— Regardless of Gender

In the summer of 1994, ESPN's directors of college sports programming—Carol Stiff and Tom Odjakjian—were trying to plug a hole. The network had an opening on Martin Luther King Day in the afternoon and wanted to find a showcase game for women's basketball. The home team was already set: Connecticut, with its senior All-American, Rebecca Lobo, which would open the season ranked fourth in the country.

NO. **24**

Their opponents were much less certain.

ESPN tried to get North Carolina—the defending national champions—to take the game. Sylvia Hatchell and the Tar Heels declined. The next call was to Louisiana Tech, which would be ranked third in the preseason poll. Leon Barmore and the Lady Techsters turned them down. Two more calls to two other teams resulted in two more rejections. Finally, needing to make the game happen, Stiff called Pat Summitt at Tennessee. Summitt's Lady Vols were the top-ranked team in the country to start the season, one year removed from a trip to the Sweet 16. Summitt was already a legend in the game, having made her reputation as a head coach who would play anyone, at any place, at any time. But Stiff's request was a non-conference road game in late January against a loaded team.

It was a tall ask.

"For the good of the game," Summitt told Stiff. "I'll take the game."

Stiff was stunned it was that easy. Then again, she shouldn't have been—that was Pat Summitt. The game was paramount. And putting Tennessee and Connecticut, the two best teams in the country, on national television via ESPN on a holiday, with no other sports to compete with was the best thing for women's basketball.

Pat Summitt, coaching legend, on December 14, 2008.

SHORT LIST

Pat Summitt Career Resume

NCAA championships	8
Final Four appearances	18
NCAA tournaments	36
Conference tournament titles	16
Conference regular-season titles	16
Wins	1,098
Coach of the Year awards	8
Olympic gold medals	1

If there was anyone who knew where the women's game had come from, it was Summitt. She was there at its infancy, when it wasn't even a sanctioned sport by the NCAA, before Title IX made it possible for women to have opportunities in college athletics. She was a part of the first-ever US Olympic women's basketball team, at the 1976 Summer Games. She was the head coach by the time the 1984 Olympics in Los Angeles rolled around, and there she led the US team to its first gold medal in history—creating the foundation that would pave the way for six more golds.

At every turn toward the future of the women's game, Summitt was there keeping it on track. Not that she would have ever taken credit for it. Before her death in 2016 at the age of 64, Summitt had established a historic career as the head coach for Tennessee. She was the face of the Lady Vols program—one of the most dominant in *any* NCAA sport—for nearly four decades. She won eight national championships, made 18 Final Four appearances, and nurtured the games of some of the best players in women's basketball history. By the time she retired in 2012, Summitt had amassed 1,098 wins—more than any Division 1 coach in NCAA history, men's *or* women's.

If there was some doubt about the magnitude of Summitt's career and her contributions to the game of women's basketball, note this: From 1976 through 2011, every player who played for her had a chance to play in at least one Final Four. That was domination on a scale few coaches in any sport, at any level, have ever enjoyed.

"For such a long time, Pat Summitt has been the gatekeeper for women's basketball," close friend and rival C. Vivian Stringer of Rutgers said when Summitt retired. "Her contributions to the game go far beyond the 1,098 victories and eight national championships. It's about the impact she has had on every Lady Vol that has come through that program to the countless others across the globe whose lives she has touched—those are things that make Pat special. She represents a pillar of strength and a source of inspiration for all of us."

Perhaps most importantly, Summitt never let women's basketball be relegated to the realm of "other sports." Women's basketball was just basketball played by women. In 2007, at the Final Four, Summitt defended the use of "Lady" before Vols in her team's name, even though some thought it was anachronistic. "That's who we are, that's how people know us," Summitt said that afternoon in Cleveland.

She was defiant in her beliefs and principles. When she was diagnosed with early-onset Alzheimer's before her final season, she still coached. According to close friend and biographer Sally Jenkins of the *Washington Post*, Summitt's response to a doctor's advice that she retire immediately upon her diagnosis was: "Do you know who you're dealing with?"

She was awarded the Presidential Medal of Freedom in 2012—the highest civilian award in the United States.

The disease eventually won, but Summitt's spirit never lost. She was awarded the Presidential Medal of Freedom in 2012—the highest civilian award in the United States. It was a symbol of her perseverance and determination to make her sport—and those playing it—better off.

That was why she said "yes" to Stiff's phone call almost 20 years earlier. Facing Connecticut on the road—the two teams would both be undefeated and ranked No. 1 and 2 in the country—was a stage that her sport couldn't afford to pass up. The game was so monumental that the release of the Associated Press Top 25 would be delayed a day to account for the result of the game.

Connecticut was victorious, knocking off Tennessee, 77–66. The Lady Vols were knocked from their undefeated perch, becoming the 13th victim in UConn's 35-win undefeated season. (The two teams would meet three months later in the national title game, with Tennessee losing, 70–64.) But the January 16 game was everything ESPN and fans of women's college basketball hoped that it would be. Except for Summitt—her team had lost. Stiff congratulated Huskies head coach Geno Auriemma, before making her way to the Tennessee locker room. There, she found Summitt standing outside the locker room, staring at the box score.

Summitt looked up at Stiff.

"For the good of the game," she said.

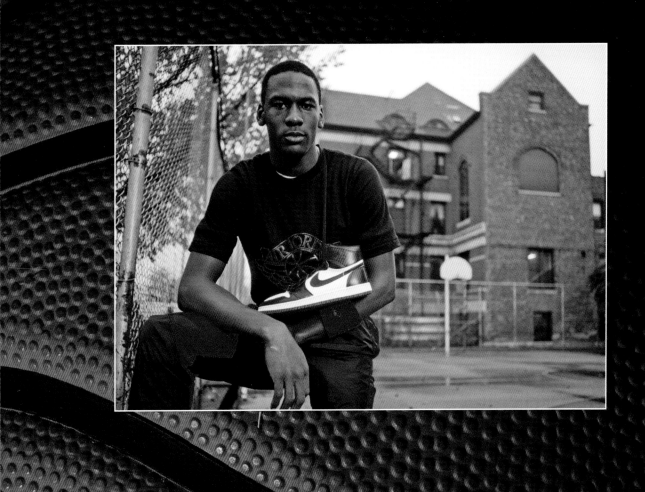

AIR JORDANS

The Business of Basketball Sneakers Goes Up, Up, and Away

It's hard to conceive of it now, but there did exist a time when Nike and basketball sneakers didn't go hand-in-hand. By 1984, Nike was still running third behind Converse and Adidas in the sneaker wars. The burgeoning company from Oregon was good at making sneakers, but not so great at getting basketball players to wear them.

So Nike watched helplessly as more and more kids continued to sport Converse's Chuck Taylor All Stars and Adidas's Jabbar or Top 10. Its plan to crack the top two of the sneaker market was this: Find a marketable superstar.

Problem was, they could hardly get a noteworthy player's attention. Nike threw a paltry sum of $8,000 a year to attract players. They got a few, but no one of note. Converse (Magic Johnson, Larry Bird, Isiah Thomas), Adidas (Kareem Abdul-Jabbar), and even New Balance (which signed James Worthy to an unheard of eight-year, $1.2 million deal after he was picked first in 1982) shelled out more. They got all the marquee names. Nike was left paying out relatively small sums of money for a lot of players who never amounted to anything. So when the 1984 NBA Draft class started to roll out, its executive team—led by Rob Strasser—had to try something new.

It fell in their laps, when an agent from Chapel Hill called to set up a meeting with a top rookie player named Michael Jordan.

"(Strasser) was an MVP in the deal," Peter Moore, another Nike executive involved in the push for Jordan, told *USA Today* in 2015. "He was the one who decided that Nike needed a basketball icon. He figured out that Nike was going nowhere in basketball which at the time was on the brink of becoming a big, big market opportunity. The inner city kid was

Michael Jordan sporting the Air Jordan I.

just beginning to become important. It all makes great sense today, 30 years later, but back then Rob's idea was thought to be risky, and so we kind of Just Did It."

Jordan had worn Converse at North Carolina, but really wanted to wear Adidas. He had meetings with both, and neither one thought he was a player worth building a campaign around—much less designing a sneaker for. Jordan's agent, David Falk, pushed Nike for action. Nike, as it turned out, was looking for just what Falk and Jordan were selling.

That is the short version of how the biggest-selling basketball sneaker—and sneaker franchise—of all time, was birthed. When the Air Jordan was introduced in time for Jordan's rookie year, they retailed for $65 a pair. Customers initially balked, but sales skyrocketed once NBA commissioner David Stern began fining Jordan for violations of the dress code (players were supposed to wear white sneakers only), grossing $130 million. The campaign to turn Jordan—and Nike—into basketball powerhouses began.

Jordan's personality allowed Nike to market a player in a way that few companies were afforded. He was handsome, a success on the court. And then there was his megawatt smile. Nike wanted to push the envelope with its commercials for the sneaker. It wanted to get away from the staid formula of player-in-gym-dunking-then-telling-you-to-buy-the-sneaker that every company did. So, it hired Spike Lee as Mars Blackmon to star and direct alongside Jordan.

The rest, again, is history.

"It was the first time Nike tried to use humor in its advertising—regardless of whether the spots were funny or not," said Jim Riswold, the commercial's copywriter for Wieden+Kennedy, the ad agency which worked on the Air Jordan campaign for Nike. "Nike advertising was no-nonsense up until then: Show the athlete sweat seriously. Furthermore, I think it showed

"On October 15th, Nike created a revolutionary new basketball shoe. On October 18th, the NBA threw them out of the game. Fortunately, the NBA can't keep you from wearing them."
—*Nike commercial following NBA's ban on Air Jordan Is*

AND ONE!

Michael as a human—warts and all. Mars was everyman and every Jordan fan could relate to Michael through Mars."

Air Jordans soon couldn't stay on the shelves. Nike had hit the jackpot.

Since the debut of the first version of the sneaker, Nike has released 30 versions of the Air Jordan. It has become its own brand, under the umbrella of Nike itself, taking in over *$2 billion annually*. It has off-shooted to include baseball, football, other Olympic sports. Entire college basketball teams—including North Carolina—have apparel deals with the Jordan brand. Even Bugs Bunny's official sneakers are Air Jordans.

"It was the player, it was the shoe, it was the success he had, it was the genius advertising that came with it," said Ben Osborne, editor-in-chief of *SLAM* magazine, and a basketball sneaker historian. "Every shoe released since, is dreaming in some way of having that moment. The Currys (from Under Armour) are hot right now. They're hoping to be the Air Jordans of today. Every Kobe release, every LeBron release, the Reebok pump—the Air Jordan set the precedent that a basketball shoe could become a phenomenon and drive conversations."

Adidas is still in the game, but controls a fraction of the market share Nike does.

More than three decades after Nike received its manna from heaven in Jordan, the company has become *the* colossus in the sneaker industry. Its challengers have all fallen by the wayside. Converse was bought by Nike in 2003. Adidas is still in the game, but controls a fraction of the market share Nike does. There have been upstarts who appeared ready to challenge the throne—Reebok (bought by Adidas in 2005) and Under Armour today—but Nike still dominates, accounting for nearly 90 percent of all basketball sneaker sales in the United States.

"It was the first shoe to be a high-performing basketball shoe that was also cool to wear off the court," Osborne said. "Every basketball sneaker since, its dream is to be seen the way the Air Jordan was seen."

Even though Jordan has been retired for nearly 15 years, his sneaker remains the must-buy item each year when the newest line is unveiled. Kids now wear his sneakers on playgrounds across the country—and the world—the way they did Chuck Taylors, even if most kids now only know of Jordan as "that guy who sells sneakers."

Only in America.

LAKERS MOVE TO LOS ANGELES

Staid Franchise Becomes the (Purple and) Gold Standard

NO. **26**

The big, hulking concrete behemoth of a building on 2nd Avenue South was empty. That's what the owner of the best damn team in professional basketball kept thinking every time his team took the floor in the old Minneapolis Auditorium. Bob Short was known as a man who valued the almighty dollar more than anything. His team—the Minneapolis Lakers—had won four of the first five NBA championships since the league debuted in 1949. Other owners in the league were envious of Short's position.

But Short cared about money. Specifically, making more of it than anyone else. So after he bought the team from its original owners, Ben Berger and Morris Chalfen, in 1957, Short began taking a look at things more closely. There was no more George Mikan—the 6'10" gentle giant who was the star of those early Laker championship teams—to draw people to the Auditorium for games. And even when the franchise drafted Elgin Baylor in 1958, it did little to get fans in the area to come to games.

So, Bob Short played the one card at his disposal: He was going to move the team.

Possible destinations included Brooklyn, Cleveland, Washington, DC, Baltimore, Pittsburgh, and San Francisco—all of whom desperately wanted to get in on the burgeoning

January 2, 1960. Coach Jim Pollard, left, talking with the Lakers during their last season in Minneapolis.

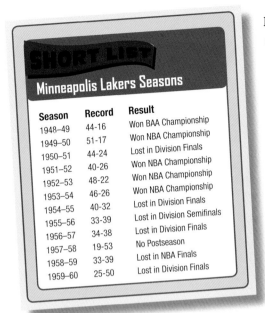

SHORT LIST

Minneapolis Lakers Seasons

Season	Record	Result
1948–49	44-16	Won BAA Championship
1949–50	51-17	Won NBA Championship
1950–51	44-24	Lost in Division Finals
1951–52	40-26	Won NBA Championship
1952–53	48-22	Won NBA Championship
1953–54	46-26	Won NBA Championship
1954–55	40-32	Lost in Division Finals
1955–56	33-39	Lost in Division Semifinals
1956–57	34-38	Lost in Division Finals
1957–58	19-53	No Postseason
1958–59	33-39	Lost in NBA Finals
1959–60	25-50	Lost in Division Finals

NBA product. But Short decided to head elsewhere. He decided to take his franchise to the one place where people would be excited to see a good team, with good players, and a good brand of basketball play night in and night out.

He went to Los Angeles, California.

"Los Angeles offers good money and an enthusiastic crowd," he told the Associated Press on Feb. 26, 1960.

It did. And it offered him the opportunity to no longer be in debt for more than $100,000, which was the scenario he was in while the team was in Minnesota. On April 28, the Minneapolis Lakers moved 1,931 miles west to become the Los Angeles Lakers—a move that not only changed the franchise, but the landscape of professional basketball.

The Lakers became a symbol for success in the NBA. After the move, the franchise slowly but surely built a rabid following. Their first title in Los Angeles wouldn't come until 1972—more than a decade after their relocation—but seven appearances in the championship series set the tone for a winning atmosphere. It also set the tone for how the NBA would structure itself.

Prior to the Lakers, there were no league teams west of the Mississippi River. In the years to come, the league would add teams in Seattle, Houston, Phoenix, and Portland. But the Lakers were the gold standard. Their teams have consistently been among the best in the NBA year after year. Since moving from Minneapolis, the franchise has missed the playoffs just seven times in 56 seasons. They have won 11 NBA titles during that time. In 2013 former NBA star and current Clippers head coach Doc Rivers called the Lakers "the best franchise in sports history." It's a hard point to argue.

The move to Los Angeles made the Lakers—and the city that was springing up around it—an "it" destination. If you were a free agent, you wanted to sign there. If you were a top player looking to get traded, you wanted to end up in LA. It was a total package: superstar players, superstar coaches, superstar owners, movie stars sitting courtside, sex appeal, and the chance to win a title every year.

And since the team arrived in California, they have enjoyed an especially lucky streak. After losing Mikan and drafting Baylor, the Lakers added Jerry West upon landing in Los Angeles. As those players' careers were ending, the team added Wilt Chamberlain and Gail Goodrich. As those players' careers began declining, the team traded for Kareem Abdul-Jabbar. Once the Lakers realized Kareem couldn't do it alone, they were put in the incredible position to draft not one, but two future Hall of Famers in a three-year span—Magic Johnson and James Worthy. When the Magic-Worthy era came to a close, the team signed Shaquille O'Neal and then pulled off a draft-day trade for Kobe Bryant.

The Lakers have become one of the most recognized brands in all of sports.

Everything seems to come up Lakers—even when it looks like it shouldn't.

"We've had so many incredible players in Los Angeles," said West—who served in the team's front office from 1982 to 2002, overseeing eight Lakers championships—in 2016. "And I know Boston's got a lot of retired jerseys up there, but I would defy you to find a franchise that had more players that have left a mark on the NBA that Laker players have had. Good fortune."

The Lakers have become one of the most recognized brands in all of sports. The franchise—in the hands of the Buss family since 1979—is worth $2.7 billion, according to a 2015 valuation done by *Forbes* magazine, making it the second-most valuable NBA franchise behind the New York Knicks. On a global scale, the Lakers are one of the top-10 most valuable sports franchises in the world, consistently ranking alongside Real Madrid, the New York Yankees, and the Dallas Cowboys.

All because of a move west to escape a dying market and a decrepit building where fans had stopped showing up to support a winning team. Bob Short cared about money—perhaps to the detriment at times of his franchise—but he saw the value in putting a good team in a blossoming market, where fans would appreciate it. Plus, when he sold the Lakers five years after the move to Los Angeles to Jack Kent Cooke, he made $5 million on the transaction.

He paid $140,000 for the team in 1957.

1985 NBA DRAFT LOTTERY

A Conspiracy Theory for the Ages Is Born

NO. **27**

"The drum will now be turned, to further mix the envelopes, and then I will conduct the drawing."

This was, potentially, David Stern's first mistake: He showed the world what he was doing. It was the afternoon of May 12, 1985, in the Starlight Roof room of the Waldorf-Astoria, and the sophomore commissioner of the National Basketball Association was getting ready to test out the league's new idea. For years, the first pick of the annual draft had been determined by getting the team with the worst record in each conference and then—being serious, here— *flipping a coin.*

No really, it's true.

Draft rights to Elvin Hayes, Lew Alcindor, and Bob Lanier? Coin flip.

Draft rights to Bill Walton and David Thompson? Coin. Flip.

Draft rights to Magic Johnson, James Worthy, Ralph Sampson, and Hakeem Olajuwon? *Coin. Freakin'. Flip.*

So when the NBA decided that the future of its latest superstar would be best determined by a lottery instead of the tossing of a coin in the air, most teams thought: "Well, it beats the alternative." So for 1985, the NBA introduced the concept of the lottery—each non-playoff team had its name placed inside an envelope and thrown into a large, plastic, see-through tumbler. The envelope pulled out first received the first pick, and so on down the line. A crude, somewhat arcane, but certainly more transparent method of determining who selected first overall.

Patrick Ewing accepts his New York Knicks jersey
after being drafted No. 1 on June 18, 1985.

Or at least, that's what Stern thought.

For as soon as he plunged his hand into the oversized beach ball–like tumbler that held the envelopes—and the futures of so many franchises (and in some sense, the NBA)—the conspiracy theories began. The consensus No. 1 pick that year was Georgetown's Patrick Ewing—a seven-foot freak of nature who had been college basketball's most intimidating and dominant player for the last four years. Every team wanted him.

There were other good players waiting to be picked in 1985—Wayman Tisdale and Benoit Benjamin were likely to be the next two off the board. Good, solid college players, but neither was Ewing. Future Hall of Famers Chris Mullin, Karl Malone, Joe Dumars, and Arvydas Sabonis would go in later picks and rounds. All-Stars Xavier McDaniel, Detlef Schrempf, A. C. Green, and Terry Porter were there too. But Ewing was *Ewing*. He was strong, fast, could block shots, make shots, and scare the hell out of you if you were heading down the middle. He was the prototype for the next generation of NBA big men.

After all seven envelopes had been plucked and placed on the board, Stern went about opening each one.

Golden State (which under the old method, would have been involved in the coin flip with Indiana). Then Sacramento. Atlanta, Seattle, and the LA Clippers. All that remained were the Pacers and the hometown New York Knicks. And if you like conspiracy theories, here is where one of the greatest in sports history was born. Stern, a lifelong New Yorker, grew up a Knicks fan, sneaking into the old Garden as a kid to watch games. The Knicks—since winning their last title in 1973—had for the most part, stunk. Sure there were six playoff appearances, but the franchise was well down the pecking order in the Eastern Conference, behind Boston, Philadelphia, and soon, Detroit and Chicago.

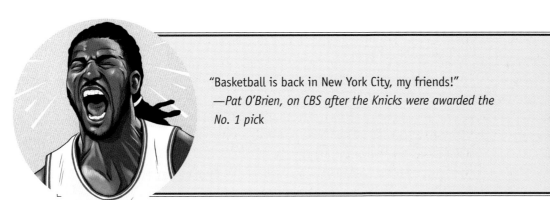

"Basketball is back in New York City, my friends!"
—*Pat O'Brien, on CBS after the Knicks were awarded the No. 1 pick*

AND ONE!

The Knicks needed Ewing. And according to some conspiracy theorists, the NBA felt the same way. In the *New York Times*, a week before the lottery, Sam Goldaper, the paper's long-time NBA writer wrote: "While the other owners participating in the lottery express similar thoughts about Ewing, there is a strong feeling among league officials and television advertising executives that the N.B.A. will benefit most if he winds up in a Knick uniform."

Stern wanted transparency about the process from the start. But as soon as CBS anchor Pat O'Brien announced that the Knicks had won the lottery, fans not wearing the blue and orange cried foul. They cried *conspiracy*.

The NBA Draft Lottery had proven to be a hit—for all the unintended reasons.

Their evidence:

- Stern fumbles around before pulling out the Knicks one!

- Even more telling—the Knicks envelope has a corner bent!

- Wait, just a minute! Doesn't the accounting guy—Jack Wagner of Ernst & Whinney, which *just so happened* to be the auditing firm for Gulf Western, which owned the Knicks by the way—pause for an extra split second before tossing the Knicks envelope in the drum?

- And here is the coup de grâce—that NBA officials had the Knicks envelope placed in a freezer, so that it would be cold to the touch and easily identified by Stern. Hence, why he fumbles around looking for it.

So . . . conspiracy?

"If people want to say that, fine," Stern told the media when questions of the outcome inevitably arose. "As long as they spell our name right. That means they're interested in us. That's terrific."

The NBA Draft Lottery had proven to be a hit—for all the unintended reasons. The Knicks took Ewing first overall the next month, and turned into a power in the Eastern Conference for the next decade and a half. (Though, fans of karma will point out they never won that title they were supposed to.) The NBA continued ahead with the lottery, eventually moving to the weighted, Ping-Pong ball system we know today, based on each team's record.

Stern, though, has never been able to escape the cries that he rigged the outcome to get Ewing to the Knicks. Repeatedly, when he has been asked about it in the three-plus decades since it happened, he has either laughed it off or blown it off. To him, the process worked better than its predecessor, and the team that was selected picked the player it was supposed to.

But the conspiracy calls have never died down.

BILL RUSSELL

Professional Basketball's Biggest Champion

It seems that the only appropriate way to broach Bill Russell as a topic of conversation is in the form of a debate. He is widely recognized as one of the very best players the game of basketball—on any level—has produced. *But how great?* He is, without a doubt, one of the greatest champions the game of basketball—on every level—has produced. *But was he just surrounded by other good players?* He is a giant in a literal and metaphorical sense, in pioneering African-American athletes in the mainstream of the sport. *But didn't others do more?*

NO.

See, there it is.

Every true statement about the career of William Felton "Bill" Russell of West Monroe, Louisiana, who was made famous in Boston, Massachusetts, by way of San Francisco, California, can be combated with another question that throws it all into a muck once again. Even Russell's place in this book is up for debate.

But if you really want to get a sense of the perplexity that is the basketball life of Bill Russell, perhaps this quote from his former teammate of nine years—Tommy Heinsohn, himself a Boston Celtics legend and Hall of Famer—will suffice. In speaking to the great sportswriter Frank Deford for a *Sports Illustrated* profile on Russell in 1999, Heinsohn said the following: "Look, all I know is, the guy won two NCAA championships, 50-some college games in a row, the (1956) Olympics, then he came to Boston and won 11 championships in 13 years and they named a f------ tunnel after Ted Williams."

Is Russell a victim of being *too* dominant?

Is Russell still overlooked because he was a star before the advent of mass media?

Player-coach Bill Russell (6) of the Boston Celtics
sinks a hook shot on October 27, 1966.

Is Russell paying the price because he stuck his finger in the eye of racists?

Maybe. Maybe not. The numbers that Russell compiled over the course of his career put him near the top of the mountain of the best players in basketball history. He was a star at McClymonds High School in Oakland, where he won two state championships as a junior and senior. He won back-to-back NCAA championships at the University of San Francisco in 1955 and 1956. After slyly being drafted by the Celtics (Red Auerbach traded veteran All-Star Ed Macauley and Cliff Hagan to the St. Louis Hawks to get the No. 2 pick in the 1956 draft), he played 13 seasons and won 11 NBA championships. Oh, and it should be mentioned that after Auerbach retired in 1966, Russell took over *coaching duties* for the final three years of his career, becoming the first black coach in league history. His record: 162-83, winning two NBA titles.

"I had been an assistant coach to Red and I was a team captain," Russell said in a 2005 live chat with fans. "So when Red got thrown out of the game, I would take over. And Red used to get thrown out of a lot of games. . . . But I think being black had nothing to do with it. I think if that was the main reason why I got the job, I probably wouldn't have taken it. I was just the best man for the job, because of my knowledge of the game, abilities and leadership skills."

At 6'9", Russell was dominant at a time in the NBA when centers could shape the way the game was played. But he also played at the same time (and some argue, in the shadow of) another dominant center: Wilt Chamberlain. The two men were immediately identified as rivals, though Russell has always stated the two were friends and competitors. While Russell was a consummate winner, Chamberlain always garnered the headlines. Chamberlain

On Battling Bill Russell

"Bill Russell helped make my dream a better dream, because when you play with the best, you know you have to play your best."—*Wilt Chamberlain*

AND ONE!

always produced eye-popping statistics, while Russell's stats—though outstanding—paled in comparison because he was surrounded by so many talented players on the Celtics. (For his 13-year career, Russell averaged 15.1 points and 22.5 rebounds per game; Chamberlain averaged 30.1 points and 22.9 rebounds over 14 seasons.)

"People thought that, for a while, we really didn't like each other," Chamberlain told NBC Sports in a joint interview special with Russell in 1997. "They always chose to believe that you could not be as good as we both were, doing our thing, and like (each other). I had to be envious of him. The only thing I was envious of him, was the fact that people—from time to time—would call me a 'loser.' And I would think, 'If I'm a loser, then damn near everyone else playing is a loser because he won all the time.'"

And that's where the legacy of Russell gets complicated. His success begs the bigger question: Why wasn't Bill Russell appreciated more?

Michael Jordan won six titles and had a statue erected outside of the United Center months after his first retirement. Magic Johnson won five titles and had a statue outside the Staples Center by 2004. Kareem Abdul-Jabbar had a statue in Los Angeles by 2012. Julius Erving had one. Jerry West—*who was denied six championships because of Russell-led teams*—had a statue unveiled in 2011.

Russell never had such a presence in Boston until 2013.

He always felt under-appreciated, despite what he accomplished in Boston. The Celtics never were a major draw at the box office when his teams were winning, especially compared to what a hot ticket the team would become in the 1980s with Larry Bird as their star. Race had a lot to do with it. In 1966, Russell told the Associated Press that a "poisoned atmosphere of hate, distrust and ignorance" hung over the city. When the Celtics retired Russell's number in 1972, he didn't attend. When he was inducted into the Hall of Fame, he didn't come.

When the Celtics retired Russell's number in 1972, he didn't attend.

That was Russell to his core though—always strident in his beliefs, even if it cost him in public perception or put another dent in his legacy. Those are things he hardly cared about. Being a champion? That something they'd never be able to take away from him.

Or debate.

THE FAB FIVE
A Murky Identity from the Very Beginning . . . and Still Going

Any conversation about the "Fab Five" should be prefaced with this caveat: They hated being called the "Fab Five."

To understand why, you have to go back to the beginning. Two years after beating Seton Hall in overtime to win the national championship, Michigan basketball was in a strange place. The Wolverines made the NCAA Tournament again in 1989-90, but lost in the second round. The next year, they lost in the first round . . . *of the NIT*. The program was not trending in the right direction. Fans and alumni expected Michigan to become a perennial basketball powerhouse, something which it had come close to doing multiple times in its past, but never could gain a foothold.

So Michigan and head coach Steve Fisher started aiming big. He and his staff began assembling a list of the high school players they felt could turn the program back to where it was a few years prior and vault the Wolverines into the conversation with Duke, North Carolina, and Kansas. The target list was ambitious:

- Chris Webber, No. 1 overall recruit nationally
- Juwan Howard, No. 3 overall recruit nationally
- Jalen Rose, No. 6 overall recruit nationally
- Jimmy King, No. 9 overall recruit nationally
- Ray Jackson, No. 84 overall recruit nationally

NO. 29

Michigan's Fab Five in November 1991: from left, Jimmy King, Juwan Howard, Chris Webber, Jalen Rose, and Ray Jackson.

And Michigan landed every one of them.

Basketball—not just college—was about to be turned on its head.

The banners from those two NCAA runner-up finishes were taken down and put into storage.

"We were almost compared to somebody like the Beatles," Howard told *USA Today* in 2002. "We used to go on the road and there'd be fans lined up outside our hotel wanting our autographs. There's be people on the campus selling t-shirts with our names on them, with our faces on them."

At a time in America when black culture and youth culture were colliding in one big, loud, angry voice, the recruiting class Michigan put together in the fall of 1991 was a perfect congregating place. College basketball, since its inception, was a place where few things changed. College players were clean-cut, wore crisp white sneakers, with clean white socks. Jerseys were always tucked in and the shorts were always thigh-high.

Michigan's new class threw a brick through that glass house.

"Five black kids starting at the University of Michigan," Fisher told *USA Today* in 2002. "That might have offended some Michigan people. Not many would admit to that fact, but it might have."

They wore long, baggy shorts. Black sneakers, black socks. The jerseys were loose and rarely tucked in. They got in your face whether you wore maize and blue or played for the other team. They were good—and they knew it. By the middle of the 1991-92 season, Fisher had no choice: He was starting all five kids. From that Sunday afternoon at Notre Dame, when Fisher started the whole group, there was no looking back. Michigan finished the season 11-3, advancing to the national championship game to play Duke—which was, in terms of public perception, the opposite of the Wolverines' brash youngsters.

As it did earlier in the season, Michigan lost to Duke—only this time it was more humiliating (71–51) and in front of the whole country.

Unlike today, the pressure to turn pro immediately wasn't in full effect. Michigan returned its entire freshman class for the 1992-93 season, with its sights set on a national championship. Michigan opened the 1992-93 season ranked No. 1 in the country. At 26-4, the Wolverines once again entered the NCAAs as the team to beat and once again, made it all the way to the national title game.

"My idea of an ideal championship game, would be to be sitting on the bench with three minutes to play," Rose told reporters ahead of the title game against North Carolina, "leading by 30 points already wearing a championship shirt."

It never happened. Down two with 11 seconds left, Webber—the team's star—dribbled into the corner in front of his team's bench. Pressured by two Carolina defenders, Webber called a timeout when the Wolverines had none. Technical foul. Game over. Championship lost. Dynasty crumbled.

The worst was yet to come, as it came out by 2000 that Michigan players—including Webber—had taken money and gifts from Ed Martin, a school booster. Michigan self-imposed sanctions on its team, but the biggest black eye was reserved for the Fab Five years: It vacated its two Final Four games in 1992 and the entire 1992-93 season. The banners from those two NCAA runner-up finishes were taken down and put into storage. As of 2016, they have yet to be re-raised.

Michigan has been reluctant to fully embrace the Fab Five in the two-plus decades since their arrival in Ann Arbor. Documentaries have been made, the players on the team have engaged in public wars of words—with the school, the NCAA, and each other—while history continues to pass them by. The closest thing to a reunion was when all five players made it to the Georgia Dome in 2013 to watch Michigan play for the national title against Louisville. Howard, Rose, King, and Jackson sat with Michigan fans in the stands. Webber sat by himself in a private suite.

The group hated the nickname bestowed on them when they arrived, preferring to be known as "5X"—"five times." They felt it was too commercial. Too mainstream. Even from the beginning, their identity was up in the air. A quarter of a century later, it seems that's still the case.

On Facing Its Nemesis Duke and All-American Christian Laettner:

"I thought Christian Laettner was an overrated p----. I really did. Until I actually got on the floor with him and realized that he had game."— *Jalen Rose,* 30 For 30: The Fab Five

AND ONE!

SHOWTIME
Lights, Cameras . . . and Redefining Basketball Action

Jerry Buss wanted a show.

In the late 1960s and into the 1970s, Buss was a budding real estate maven around the Los Angeles area. He would routinely hit up a trendy nightclub in nearby Santa Monica called The Horn. It was a Wilshire Boulevard–type place, filled with rich people, looking to get seen and see others. Musicians, comedians, and entertainers would play the joint, but the opening act always began like this—the lights would dim, until the single spotlight would find the house entertainer placed at one of the tables, who would stand up and belt the club's signature song:

It's showtiiiiiiiiiiiiiiiiiiiime! It's showwwwwwwwwwwwwwwtiiiiiiiiiiiiiiiiiiiiiiime!

Buss would look around and watch the crowd coo and holler. He saw the excitement that phrase could bring to a room. So when he bought the Los Angeles Lakers and the building they played in—The Forum—in 1979, Buss immediately was transported back to his private booth at The Horn. He wanted to replicate it. He wanted the excitement, the tingle you got when you heard that phrase. The hint of sex, and money, and fame, and power, all swirling together in one place. He wanted the atmosphere of The Horn on a grand scale.

He wanted *Showtime*.

"It was simply, the NBA at its most fun," recalled Mark Heisler, who covered the Lakers for the *Los Angeles Times* during that era. "There was nothing like it."

During Buss's initial years owning the flagship franchise of the NBA, the Lakers went from being a dominant team in the league to being *the* show in all of sports. With charismatic

Actor Jack Nicholson sits courtside for NBA
playoff action between the Los Angeles Lakers
and the Dallas Mavericks in 1988.

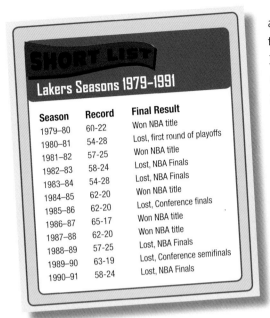

SHORT LIST

Lakers Seasons 1979–1991

Season	Record	Final Result
1979–80	60-22	Won NBA title
1980–81	54-28	Lost, first round of playoffs
1981–82	57-25	Won NBA title
1982–83	58-24	Lost, NBA Finals
1983–84	54-28	Lost, NBA Finals
1984–85	62-20	Won NBA title
1985–86	62-20	Lost, Conference finals
1986–87	65-17	Won NBA title
1987–88	62-20	Won NBA title
1988–89	57-25	Lost, NBA Finals
1989–90	63-19	Lost, Conference semifinals
1990–91	58-24	Lost, NBA Finals

and talented players like Magic Johnson, James Worthy, Kareem Abdul-Jabbar, Michael Cooper, Norm Nixon, Byron Scott, Kurt Rambis—and a cast of dozens more over a decade-long run—and a sharp, slick head coach in Pat Riley, the team became must-see-TV every night. The "Showtime" moniker stuck to the style of play the Lakers put together—a quick-rebound, quick-pass, run-up-the-floor-and-score method of offense, a high-wire act in basketball sneakers.

But more than that, the Lakers' decade of "Showtime" became quintessential LA.

The Forum—later renamed the Great Western Forum—transformed into the hottest nightclub in town. Figuratively . . . and literally. Celebrities would flock from all corners of Los Angeles, Hollywood, Santa Monica, and Beverly Hills to sit courtside at Lakers games. Frenzied fans would line up for tickets to see the best team in professional basketball—and maybe catch a glimpse of Jack Nicholson. Or Dyan Cannon. Or Michael Jackson. Or Arsenio Hall. Or Paula Abdul (after she moved up from being a Laker Girl). "Sitting courtside" became the Ciro's of 1980s Hollywood—the ultimate place to be seen.

"I thought, 'Wouldn't it be great if I could always have movie stars, consistently, at the Forum?'," Buss told the *Los Angeles Times* in 1986. "Eventually, everyone would know if you really want to see a movie star, there would be one place you could do it: Jerry Buss's box at the Forum."

And when the game was over, the party would just begin. As part of his deal with Jack Kent Cooke to purchase the team, the jewel that struck Buss's eye the most—he was a real estate man, after all—was The Forum. Attached to it was the Forum Club, a family-friendly joint built by Cooke for fans to grab a meal after the game was over. It was a rather drab, nondescript place. Buss changed that too. He made the Forum Club into the hottest nightclub in Los Angeles. There was a private entrance for celebrities, players, families—and on most nights, women as far as the eye could see.

"That was the only real VIP club at an arena at the time," Josh Rosenfeld, the Lakers's public relations director during the 1980s told ESPN.com in 2011. "I would get just as many requests for passes to the Forum Club than I would get for tickets to the game. Especially after the game it was a big deal. To be able to get dinner at the Forum Club was a really big deal. It was a private club that only certain season-ticket holders were able to purchase memberships to. It was as hot a commodity as tickets."

Everyone wanted to be around the Lakers. It was not hard to see why. Magic was among the most genial personas in Los Angeles, routinely dazzling sellout crowds with a never-empty bag of tricks. Kareem was nearing his final years on the court, but still was a force—and a legend—who was more aloof, but still a thrill to be around for many. Worthy was quickly becoming one of the best players in the league.

With Riley running the ship, the Lakers dominated the NBA once again. From the arrival of Magic before the 1979-80 season through the 1990-91 season, the Lakers won 712 of their 984 regular-season games; won the Pacific Division 10 times; won the Western Conference title nine times; and won five NBA titles.

That would have been a large enough legacy to leave in its own right. But Showtime went beyond just the product on the court.

What sports fans enjoy (or in some cases, loathe) nightly at sporting venues is due in large part to the atmosphere Buss created. Music between breaks in play. Celebrities sitting in expensive seats. (It is not a coincidence that when Riley took over the Knicks in 1991, Madison Square Garden saw an uptick in celebrities sitting in courtside seats.) Dancing girls. Luxury boxes. In-arena entertainment spots.

Music between breaks in play. Celebrities sitting in expensive seats. Dancing girls. Luxury boxes. In-arena entertainment spots.

"That's all Buss's vision of making the NBA entertainment, not merely sport," Jeff Perlman, author of *Showtime: Magic, Kareem, Riley and the Los Angeles Lakers Dynasty of the 1980s* told *GQ* in 2014. "He was the first to see it. Pure genius."

The Lakers had success after the 80s, when Kobe Bryant, Shaquille O'Neal, and Phil Jackson rekindled the spirits of the past. It was close, but not the real thing. Showtime was a like a comet that had burned for a short period of time, then disappeared in the night sky, never to be seen again.

But did it ever burn bright.

"Superstardom was not so big back then," Heisler said. "It was fun being around those guys, because they were fun."

LARRY O'BRIEN
Putting His Stamp on the NBA

Call it fate. Call it a strange coincidence. Call it foreshadowing. But the future commissioner of the National Basketball Association—the one who oversaw major rule changes, helped enact sweeping policies to help save the league from itself, grew the game, and orchestrated a merger to eliminate its strongest competition—was born on July 7, 1917, in, of all places, Springfield, Massachusetts.

NO. 31

The home of Lawrence Francis O'Brien Jr. would also be the place where his legacy was enshrined 74 years later.

It seemed that O'Brien was destined to end up back in the town where he was born. His career path made the route home more circuitous, but also added pieces to his public profile that helped make O'Brien the NBA's first strong-handed commissioner, and the man for whom the league's championship trophy is now named. His predecessor, J. Walter Kennedy, had served for 12 seasons taking over for the likable Maurice Podoloff in 1963. However, Kennedy's leadership style was direct and often blunt. Yes, he grew the league from nine to 18 teams before his retirement, helped orchestrate television contracts that brought money in to franchises, and helped increase attendance. But he didn't make many friends, and by the end of his tenure sensed a change needed to be made.

Enter, O'Brien—a politician in the truest sense of the word—who would help steer the league toward a path that would eventually lead to it being the billion-dollar business it is today.

"When I first got a phone call at my office in Washington asking if I were interested in the job, I wasn't," O'Brien said in a 1978 interview with the *Ocala* (FL) *Star-Banner*. "I

NBA commissioner Larry O'Brien poses with the
NBA World Championship Trophy in 1977.

had no sports experience or background. I was simply another American sports fan. I had a particular love and affection for the game of basketball, but that was it."

O'Brien had always operated in the Beltway realm of DC politics. A close friend of John F. Kennedy's, O'Brien helped set up the Massachusetts congressman's successful run for the US Senate in 1952. Eight years later, he was tasked with helping get Kennedy elected—and when that happened, he moved inside the White House, becoming the President's special assistant for congressional relations.

The Bay Stater had a particular knack for being in the right place at the right time. After Kennedy's assassination, he was folded into Lyndon Johnson's inner circle and was appointed US postmaster general in 1965. When Johnson ran for re-election in 1968, O'Brien ran the campaign. After Johnson's election, O'Brien had gained serious credibility as a person who knew how Washington politicians thought and how the electorate saw them, which got him elected the head of the Democratic National Committee. That put him in the center of the most incredible political cover-up in US history—because when burglars entered the Watergate Hotel on June 17, 1972, O'Brien was their target.

What does all of this have to do with O'Brien's foray into the NBA? Simple: He was a man who had become an expert at dealing with calamities and problems. And when he was elected to the post in April of 1975, the NBA had become a place where calamities and problems popped up daily.

"If you can remember the state of the NBA when he came in as commissioner and where we are today, you realize the fantastic job Larry has done," Portland Trail Blazers owner Larry Weinberg told the *New York Times* in 1983 after O'Brien's retirement was announced.

On Leaving the NBA after His Tenure as Commissioner

"I think the eight and one-half years I spent as commissioner was the longest I have ever spent concentrating on a particular situation or subject. If you told me eight and a half years ago when I came in, that I'd be standing here today, I wouldn't have believed it for a minute."—*Larry O'Brien,* New York Times

AND ONE!

O'Brien had to hit fastballs right from the get-go. He helped settled the antitrust lawsuit that Oscar Robertson had filed against the league, the result of which paved the way for the modern free-agency rules. He guided the merger with the NBA's chief rival—the American Basketball Association—in 1976, bringing aboard four franchises, buying out two, and leaving one to fold. In one of his final acts as commissioner, he oversaw the introduction of a salary cap, which helped give the league's smaller-market teams the sustainability to continue to operate.

The biggest piece of change O'Brien oversaw had to do with what players were using away from the court: drugs. By the late 1970s and early 80s, cocaine use was rampant in team locker rooms. A 1980 story in the *Los Angeles Times* said that as many as 75 percent of NBA players were using cocaine. O'Brien had already bolstered attendance numbers to record levels during his tenure, but saw a league that was perceived as drug-riddled as a threat to that.

In a move that was hailed as one of the strongest stances against drugs in the country, the NBA passed a rule in 1983 that any player who was convicted of, or pled guilty to, a crime involving heroin or cocaine would be banned from the league for life. A drug testing program was also instituted and players who tested positive were banned for life. "The message we are sending out today is clear: drugs and the NBA do not mix," O'Brien said at a news conference that day.

Labor peace—through a good relationship with player's union general counsel Larry Fleisher—was also a hallmark of the O'Brien era.

. . . any player who was convicted of, or pled guilty to, a crime involving heroin or cocaine would be banned from the league for life.

"Larry became commissioner at a difficult time, when everybody was suing everybody else," New York Knicks executive Dave DeBusschere told the *New York Times* upon O'Brien's retirement. "He was the one individual that helped stabilize the sport."

His tenure was among the briefest of the five commissioners the league has known, but at the time was the most influential. By the time O'Brien left his post before the 1984-85 season, the league was beginning what many believe is its golden era. That would take place under the watchful eye of a man O'Brien had hired in 1978 to be the league's general counsel. The New York City–born lawyer was smart and savvy. O'Brien thought he had the perfect demeanor to become his successor down the road.

His name was David Stern.

DUKE-NORTH CAROLINA RIVALRY

The Battle for Tobacco Road

The route is a pretty simple one: Turn left onto Science Drive, then turn right onto Cameron Boulevard; from there you've got to merge onto Route 501 South for just about nine miles; then you turn right onto Manning Drive, before making a quick left onto Skipper Bowles Drive. That's it. Five steps. A total of 10.8 miles, which—without traffic—should take you just about 20 minutes to complete.

Durham to Chapel Hill.

Or, rather: Duke University to the University of North Carolina.

That is how close the two fiercest rivals in the sport of college basketball are to one another. If you really wanted to, you could walk the distance between Duke's Cameron Indoor Stadium and Carolina's Dean E. Smith Center and do it in under four hours. For nearly 100 years, the Blue Devils and the Tar Heels have made this trip twice a year during the regular season. The Tobacco Triangle is the hub of college hoops—and in particular, the Atlantic Coast Conference—with North Carolina State located just about an hour south in Raleigh. But no two schools occupying the same air space operate at such a high level year in and year out.

How hated are these two blue blood brothers?

"I have said very publicly, that if Duke was playing against the Taliban," Congressman Brad Miller (North Carolina Class of 1975) told the Associated Press in 2012, "then I'd have to pull for the Taliban."

And if you're thinking that surely must be a misprint, because no politician would

The hardwood action of one of college sports' greatest rivalries.

ever go on the record and say that in a public setting—think again. Miller stuck by his guns. Twice. So it's not hard to see how that type of furor can ignite passions throughout the state when these two schools get together.

"Carolina has a huge following in the state, because it's a state school, while Duke has a following from all over the place," said CBS Sports analyst Jim Spanarkel, himself a former Duke player. "People who live there who are Duke fans, work alongside Carolina fans. And Carolina fans will have to show up every day with Duke fans. It's a true rivalry. It's crazy. There's no other way to cut it."

When Spanarkel—a kid from Jersey City who was recruited to come to Durham for the Blue Devils by Bill Foster in the late 1970s—first arrived at Duke, he had heard about some of the stories of the rivalry game. How the games against N.C. State and Maryland and Wake Forest were fierce, but nothing compared to the Carolina game. How in the weeks and days leading up to the games, it was all anyone talked about.

After a brief five-year run in the NBA, Spanarkel began a career as a financial planner for Merrill Lynch in northern New Jersey. Every now and then, he would come in contact with a client or business associate who would tell him they went to Carolina. That comment was usually followed up by some variation of, "And I called you everything under the sun when you played us."

"One of my best friends growing up was Mike O'Koren," Spanarkel recalled. "Mike obviously went to Carolina. Well, we'd see each other after games and hang out and people from both sides would be angry about it. To each other, it was two friends catching up. To anyone else, it was fraternizing with the enemy."

The game has transcended college basketball. The two regular-season meetings between Duke and North Carolina have become appointment television. (On the 20 occasions when the two schools have faced off in the ACC Tournament, the same holds true.) It's become so big that ESPN—which has the television rights deal for the ACC—has created a "Rivalry Week," centered around the Duke-Carolina game.

The NBA alums that sit courtside when these two get together? Too numerous to list.

As two of the premier programs in the country, Duke and North Carolina are constantly competing for more than just eyeballs. Recruiting wars often are as fierce and nastier than any regular-season game. The coaches—Mike Krzyzewski of Duke and Roy Williams of Carolina—are two of the most iconic in the game. The NBA alums that sit courtside when these two get together? Too numerous to list.

"Our games against North Carolina over the decades have proven to stand that test of greatness and time and excellence," Krzyzewski said in an interview with the ACC Network in 2014. "Whatever thing you want to check, whatever you need to have it be a great rivalry, Duke and Carolina check all the boxes."

There is one box though, that has not been checked off by either program. They have won multiple national titles since 1980—four for Carolina, to five for Duke—but have yet to find themselves matched up in the NCAA Tournament. For fans of either side, it's the final frontier: Could the biggest rivalry in the sport survive the pressure cooker of a do-or-die NCAA Tournament game? A Final Four? *A national championship?*

"You almost have to wonder, if that happened, how would it affect the rest of the country?" Spanarkel said, smirking as he pondered the thought of a Tobacco Road national title game. "The venues—the Dean Dome and Cameron—they add a lot of mystique to that rivalry, too. Move that away, and even the ACC games are usually in Greensboro (NC), so it's close, but it would be interesting to see what would happen."

Krzyzewski has been on the record saying he hopes it never comes to fruition because one half of the rivalry's fan base would be supremely crushed by the outcome—and it could poison what is a unique part of college basketball.

Still, it's fun to dream, right?

Well, maybe for those of us who aren't Duke or North Carolina fans.

On the Passions of the Duke–North Carolina Rivalry

"To legions of otherwise reasonable adults, it is a conflict that surpasses sports; it is locals against outsiders, elitists against populists, even good against evil . . . . The rivalry may be a way of aligning oneself with larger philosophic ideals—of choosing teams in life—a tradition of partisanship that reveals the pleasures and even the necessity of hatred."—*Will Blythe (a North Carolina alum)*, To Hate Like This Is to Be Happy Forever: A Thoroughly Obsessive, Intermittently Uplifting, and Occasionally Unbiased Account of the Duke–North Carolina Basketball Rivalry

AND ONE!

PHOG ALLEN

A Bridge from the Beginning to the Present

Forrest Clare "Phog" Allen set foot on the campus of the University of Kansas in the fall of 1904. He was already considered a prodigy in the new and growing game of "Basket Ball." At the age of 10, he formed a local team with his brothers. Under the rules of the game at the time, a team could only designate one player to shoot free throws, and Phog was that player. So when he arrived in Lawrence from his home two hours north in Jamesport, Missouri, Allen was intent on playing for the school's team.

NO. 33

After all, what better place to play and learn the game than at a university where the team was coached by the man who invented basketball—Dr. James Naismith.

But by all accounts Naismith was a hands-off coach. He did not employ strategy or tactics, he simply let the players do what their abilities allowed them to. From the moment Allen arrived on campus, there was a different air about him. He was more cerebral, more of a thinker about the game. Which was a perfect fit for Kansas, who were simply an average team before Allen arrived to play for them—they had never won more than seven games in a single season.

"You don't coach this game, Forrest, you play it," Naismith once told his pupil.

Naismith immediately identified Allen as a player who had a gift for coaching. In Allen's sophomore year, the Jayhawks enjoyed their best campaign yet under Naismith—12 wins, seven losses. It was official: Allen was big-time coaching material. So much so, that before the 1905-06 season began, Baker University—a school 30 minutes south of Lawrence—offered Allen the chance to be their head coach, while still playing for Kansas.

University of Kansas coach Forrest C. "Phog" Allen explains play formations to players on December 27, 1940.

He took the job for three years, while continuing to play for Kansas. By the time he left, he had amassed a 45-9 record. Allen left for good reason: Before the start of his senior season, Naismith announced he was retiring and handing the team over to Allen. He had clearly shown his ability to lead a team, to instruct where instruction was needed, while also developing a strategy to win games. Plus, it was clear that he was fast becoming a coaching junkie: In 1907-08, he coached both Baker and Kansas (compiling a 31-12 combined record); the next year, he left Baker, but took the head coaching position at Haskell Indian Nations University in Lawrence, in addition to Kansas. His combined record that year? 52-8.

In his 37 seasons as the head coach of the Jayhawks, Allen touched seemingly every important figure in the game—either directly or indirectly.

After that double-duty season though, Allen abruptly stepped away. He was still young and wanted to study osteopathic medicine. He kept his coaching juices flowing, coaching the Warrensburg Teachers College for seven seasons, leaving after the 1918-19 campaign. He had made a good career of practicing medicine and coaching basketball on the side, but something was still missing. He knew what it was: Kansas.

Suddenly Allen went from being a fanatic pupil of the inventor of the game to being the bridge that connects Naismith to the game today.

Upon his return to Lawrence in 1919, Allen almost immediately became coaching royalty. In his 37 seasons as the head coach of the Jayhawks, Allen touched seemingly every important figure in the game—either directly or indirectly. Naismith's decision to turn the Kansas team over to Allen is essentially the big bang of basketball. Over his career at Kansas, Allen coached Dutch Lonborg, Ralph Miller, Adolph Rupp, and Dean Smith. Rupp coached Pat Riley at Kentucky; Riley helped bring about the careers of Jeff and Stan Van Gundy, Kurt Rambis, Doc Rivers, Byron Scott, and Erik Spoelstra.

At North Carolina, Smith nurtured Larry Brown, Roy Williams, and George Karl; Brown, in turn, helped launch the careers of John Calipari, Gregg Popovich, Maurice Cheeks, Mike Woodson, and Kevin Ollie; Popovich gave professional birth to Brett Brown, Avery Johnson, and Mike Brown.

It is the most sprawling family tree in all of basketball, one where the current head coach of the San Antonio Spurs—widely regarded as the smartest mind in the game—can directly be traced back to the man who invented it. It's only made possible by Allen.

The branches of Allen's tree include players too. Allen recruited a 7'1" gentle giant from the Overbrook section of Philadelphia—Wilt Chamberlain—to come all the way out to Kansas to play collegiately. Three-time NBA champion Clyde Lovellette was an Allen player. So was

Bill "Skinny" Johnson, and 1923 player of the year Paul Endacott. Another Allen recruit turned out to be better in the court, than on it: former US senator Bob Dole.

Allen coached Kansas until the end of the 1955-56 season, when he hit the magic age of 70. That was, at the time, the mandatory retirement age for all state employees, and so the winningest basketball coach in college history was forced into premature retirement. Many believed that Allen, given his stature and accomplishments at Kansas (the team had won the national championship just four years earlier), would be able to fend off the state law.

It was a rare defeat for a man who didn't suffer many of them.

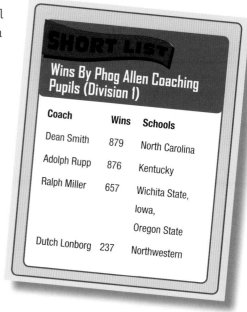

SHORT LIST

Wins By Phog Allen Coaching Pupils (Division 1)

Coach	Wins	Schools
Dean Smith	879	North Carolina
Adolph Rupp	876	Kentucky
Ralph Miller	657	Wichita State, Iowa, Oregon State
Dutch Lonborg	237	Northwestern

EUROPEAN INVASION

New Talent Comes Ashore—and Changes the Game

NO. **34**

The signs were there—and had been—for years.

Beginning in the mid-1980s and continuing for the next decade, they would appear like comets on the rosters of NBA teams with bold streaks and creative general managers. There would be tales of grainy footage, followed up by quotes of projected greatness from some basketball junkie who heard from a guy who heard from a guy who heard from a guy, who played against him in the such-and-such Olympics, and he was *uh-may-zing*. NBA teams dipping their toes in the pool of foreign talent was nothing new by this point, but the successes were few and far between. The game being played by Magic Johnson and Larry Bird and Michael Jordan was wildly different than the game being played in Spain, Turkey, or Croatia.

These guys were fantastic when the jerseys had "Real Madrid" or "Benetton Treviso" or "PAOK" on the front. But when it was the Bulls or the Pistons or the Knicks? These urban legends from continental Europe and other parts unknown always seemed to shrink to the background.

Until "The Wave" happened.

Detlef Schrempf. Rik Smits. Drazen Petrovic. Sarunas Marciulionis. Vlade Divac. Dino Rada. Gheorghe Muresan. Toni Kukoc. Zan Tabak. Arvydas Sabonis. For a decade, these stars of the grainy tapes shot in smoke-filled Euro arenas turned out to be the blockbusters the game was looking for. These weren't just Europeans coming over to try their hand at the

German Mavericks star Dirk Nowitzki on October 9, 2009.

SHORT LIST

Best European-Born NBA Players

Player	Country	Teams
Dirk Nowitzki	Germany	Mavericks
Tony Parker	France	Spurs
Pau Gasol	Spain	Grizzlies, Lakers, Bulls
Peja Stojakovic	Croatia	Kings, Pacers, Hornets, Raptors, Mavericks
Drazen Petrovic	Croatia	Trail Blazers, Nets
Detlef Schrempf	West Germany	Mavericks, Pacers, SuperSonics, Trail Blazers
Toni Kukoc	Croatia	Bulls, 76ers, Hawks, Bucks
Vlade Divac	Serbia	Lakers, Hornets, Kings
Rik Smits	Netherlands	Pacers
Arvydas Sabonis	Lithuania	Trail Blazers

NBA and eventually settling in to an eighth-man spot before heading back overseas. No, this was the crop of talent that came over and turned into bona fide NBA stars for their teams. And while some were better than others, they convinced all the NBA franchises that if you weren't looking for talent over there—well, you were going to be left behind.

Pretty soon, European players became a trend—even ahead of drafting American high schoolers.

"Perhaps the biggest factor in the rapid improvement of international players, especially in Europe, is the developmental system," longtime NBA head coach Mike D'Antoni told the *New York Daily News* in 2002. "Promising players are steered to club teams in their early teens, playing against pros, in many cases, and practicing in the same program virtually year-round. With no NCAA-mandated restrictions on practice time, no high school or college systems in place, players get a huge head start."

Why didn't the European players become NBA stars sooner? Perhaps they simply hadn't caught up to the American game. Those first initial probes may not have produced the results the teams or players had been hoping for, but it sent players back to their home leagues and countries with a definitive understanding of what NBA life was like. Pretty soon, as the league grew larger and expanded its borders internationally—both in person, on television, and through the Olympics—European players caught up. Rapidly.

In 1992, one player—Predrag Danilovic of Yugoslavia—was selected in the draft, going in the second round. By 1996, four Europeans were selected in the *first round*. By 2001, Pau Gasol of Spain was picked third overall. By 2003, seven-foot Serbian center Darko Milicic became the highest Euro player drafted—going No. 2 overall and ahead of two future Hall of Famers and an All-Star: Carmelo Anthony, Chris Bosh, and Dwyane Wade. He was one of seven European players selected in the first round. In 2006, Italy's Andrea Bargnani became the first European player picked first overall, just 21 years after Schrempf entered the league.

The push and influx of European talent came to a head during the 2006-07 season, when Germany's Dirk Nowitzki—arguably the most talented player the continent has produced—won the NBA's Most Valuable Player Award, becoming the first European player to do so. (Hakeem Olajuwon of Nigeria and Steve Nash of Canada had previously broken the award's foreign barrier.) Basketball officially had become an international game.

"It's a procedure that has taken 20 years and Dirk is the final step," Maurizio Gherardini, a longtime general manager for some of Europe's top club teams told the *Washington Post* during Nowitzki's MVP season. "It would be the ultimate step of the original baby steps for guys like Kukoc, Petrovic, Sabonis."

As the success stories have been told and teams continue to find diamonds in the rough, European players have been at the forefront of the NBA's international movement. Ahead of the 2015-16 season, the league released its annual breakdown of international talent. Exactly 100 players from 37 countries and territories were on league rosters on opening night—47 of them came from Europe. Less than a year later, at the draft in June, nine European players went in the first round.

Part of the allure is the difference in style from the American game—NBA teams know that a 6'11" post player who steps out and makes 3-pointers can cause matchup problems. Another is that drafting a European player doesn't cost anything. Teams that are loaded or jammed up with contracts or against the salary cap can still make a pick and let the player develop for a few years before deciding whether or not to bring him over. Some have criticized that practice, but for teams like the San Antonio Spurs—who have used it as well as anyone in the NBA—it has paid off.

The push and influx of European talent came to a head during the 2006-07 season, when Germany's Dirk Nowitzki . . . won the NBA's Most Valuable Player Award . . .

Not every player has been a resounding success. Bargnani has never lived up to his selection, much like Nikoloz Tskitishvili—who went fifth to the Denver Nuggets in 2002—or Frederic Weis before him. Like every talent scouting trend to hit the NBA, there have been hits and misses.

But there is no turning back now. European players are no longer a "trend." They are here to stay—and to star. The first wave of talent laid the groundwork for the next collection to come through and become superstars. What's next? Only time will tell.

NANCY LIEBERMAN JOINS THE USBL

"Lady Magic" Arrives on a Big Stage

When the announcement was made, it had the making of just another gimmick in a long, long line of them.

As soon as the United States Basketball League was formed in 1985, it had to do something—anything, really—to make it stand out from its big brother. The NBA had already swallowed up the American Basketball Association a decade earlier, so the USBL needed to stay ahead of the game in order to keep playing it. And in a league that featured washed-up pros, guys who were never quite good enough to make it to the NBA, and franchises that folded nearly as quickly as they popped up, the USBL stuck to a pretty simple marketing technique: Be different.

The league attracted a 7'7" Sudanese import who had played one season for tiny, Division II University of Bridgeport to join the league. His name? Manute Bol. There wasn't much concern if Bol could or couldn't play; the Rhode Island Gulls only cared that 1,800 people came out to every one of his home games in college.

That same inaugural year, the same Rhode Island Gulls team took a kid who had played two years at a junior college before transferring to North Carolina State. At 5'7", most scouts thought he was a better fit for the Harlem Globetrotters than professional basketball. His name? Spud Webb.

Old Dominion's Nancy Lieberman (10) takes the ball away from Louisiana Tech's Angela Turner in 1979.

One team now had the tallest player in the league and the shortest. You see how the USBL operated.

So fast-forward to June of 1986 when the defending champion of the league's first season—the Springfield Fame, based out of Massachusetts—put out an announcement that grabbed everyone's attention. The Fame had signed Nancy Lieberman.

A woman. To play professional basketball. With men.

"I remembered thinking at the time, 'A girl on the team? This has got to be another publicity stunt,'" recalled Billy Goodwin, a member of that Springfield Fame team. "All the guys had the same reaction—that it just had to be a publicity stunt. Nancy, to her credit, never treated it like a publicity stunt. When she got here, she was like, 'Hey, I can play.'"

Nancy Lieberman was, simply put, the best basketball player the women's game had ever seen. During her four years at Old Dominion, Lieberman blew away the competition. Her teams won back-to-back AIAW national championships in her junior and senior years, after winning the Women's NIT in her sophomore campaign. She was a three-time All-American, set school and national records, and was a two-time selection to the US women's Olympic basketball team in 1976 and 1980.

The highest praise? She had earned the nickname, "Lady Magic."

But in the early 1980s, the careers of great women's basketball players ended when they graduated college. She played with the Dallas Diamonds of the Women's Professional Basketball League, but it folded after her first season. She played with the foil of the Globetrotters, the Washington Generals, but it really wasn't what Lieberman had been trained for.

The Lieberman experiment lasted only one season, but the message had been sent.

She was a tough kid from Brooklyn, playing pickup games at some of the highest-profile playgrounds in the city, including Rucker Park. Lieberman would roll up to the court, looking for a game, get laughed at, then finally be allowed to play and leave her male opponents slack-jawed.

"These guys would look at me and they'd go, 'Little girl, are you lost?'" Lieberman wrote for the website *The Players Tribune* in 2015. "'I heard you guys are really good, and I want to play against guys who are really good. And I ain't afraid of you.'"

Nor was she when the USBL came calling.

She made the league maximum because of her notoriety—$10,000 a season, before taxes—but it wasn't about the paycheck. Lieberman knew there was a sideshow aspect to her arrival in the USBL, but she didn't care. This was an opportunity to play against men. Good men. To show that she wasn't just good at beating up opponents in the women's game.

"I remember when she first got to practice, we'd knock her around," said Goodwin, who has remained a friend for over 30 years. "She got up every time. Pretty soon, she wasn't a gimmick anymore. She was just 'Nancy.' She was proving that she wasn't here because it was good publicity for the team and the USBL—which I'm sure that was a part of it. She could hoop. And she insisted that we treat her like one of the guys. Even if guys still thought she was just a publicity stunt, Nancy had that character that just wore on you. After a while, you saw her as Nancy. As part of the group."

The Lieberman experiment lasted only one season, but the message had been sent. She had broken a barrier that never had been cracked before the summer of 1986. After the season ended, she played on a summer league team sponsored by the Utah Jazz. Her foray into the league encouraged the Staten Island Stallions to draft Cheryl Miller out of college.

More than breaking barriers, Lieberman's biggest contribution might be fitting in with an already talented and cohesive team. The Fame were one of the elite franchises in the USBL. Goodwin had been a star on the legendary St. John's teams in the 1980s. Fellow backcourt mate Michael Adams would go on to play 11 years in the NBA. Oliver Lee starred at Marquette.

They had been skeptical at first, but their tune quickly changed. Goodwin recalled a night when the Fame played the Wildwood Aces at Convention Hall in Atlantic City, New Jersey. Stewart Granger and Othell Wilson had been egging Lieberman on all night long.

"They asked me before the game, 'Y'all for real playing with a girl?'" Goodwin remembered. "I said, 'You bet.' And she scorched them. Just scorched them. At the end of the game, Stewart came up to me and said, 'Man, she can play!' And I said to him, 'I told you.'"

On Nancy Lieberman Joining the Springfield Fame:

"She has fit in very well. Sometimes we forget she is a lady, she fits in so well. We love her like a sister. We all look out for her, although she doesn't need us to. Whatever publicity she gets, we all benefit from it."—*Oliver Lee,* Philadelphia Inquirer

AND ONE!

JULIUS ERVING

Basketball's First High-Wire Act for the Highlight Age

You've seen it. Don't even pretend like you haven't. And if by some act of God, you've been living under a rock for the past three-and-a-half decades—with no access to a phone, television, or Internet, with which to hear about it or see it—you should really go and ask someone. The query won't even take long. All you've got to do is find a basketball fan and ask them about "The Dr. J play."

NO. 36

The first reaction you'll receive (if it's not laughter for not having seen it already yourself) is a facial expression that lies somewhere between biting into a lemon and stubbing your toe. Then, you're likely to hear the following:

"Unbelievable."

"Incredible."

"Best play I've ever seen."

Hyperbole, it is not. For that is what made Julius Winfield Erving II the pioneer of the high-air basketball highlight. While others throughout the history of the sport have been defined by their greatness, Erving—while also being defined by that label—was simply described by adjectives. When he arrived in the American Basketball Association in 1971, the sport was played on the ground. So, when Erving decided he'd rather play it in the air . . . well, you can see just how that turned the game on its ear.

"No one has ever controlled and conquered the air above pro basketball like Julius Erving, the incomparable Dr. J," sportswriter Pete Axthelm once wrote in *Newsweek*. "The

Julius Erving, star forward for the New York Nets,
poses prior to a 1974 game.

Doctor not only leaps and stays aloft longer than most players dream possible, but he uses his air time to transform his sport into graceful ballet, breath-taking drama or science-fiction fantasy, depending upon his mood of the moment and the needs of his team."

At 6'7", Erving was the precursor of the "tweener" position in today's basketball: too small to be a power forward, too big to be a shooting guard. He was a man without a position when he became a member of the Virginia Squires in 1971, but it quickly became evident that Erving's position would be above the rim. He had an incredible vertical leap, and during a time when the sport of basketball was still grounded in basic fundamental play, Erving took advantage of the holes in defenses where no one stood—and simply went up, over, or through them.

In the free-flowing ABA, he was the poster child for what the league wanted to be. Confined to rudimentary play during his college days at the University of Massachusetts because dunking had been outlawed in the NCAA, Erving found an expressive home in the burgeoning league. After financial troubles forced the Squires to sell off the Doctor to the New York Nets, Erving truly soared into the basketball consciousness of the country. It was at the inaugural Slam Dunk Contest during the 1976 ABA All-Star Game in Denver where Erving showed the game what he was capable of. In a field consisting of David Thompson, Artis Gilmore, George Gervin, and Larry Kenon, Erving took off from the free throw line and slammed it home.

The highlights of the dunk contest—and Erving's exploits in winning it—were shown all over morning shows on television the next day. America had its next basketball superstar, a player to share the mantle with Kareem Abdul-Jabbar and continue the game's rich legacy of otherworldly talent. And Erving's star was about to get bigger, as the ABA merged with the NBA in time for the 1976-77 season: Dr. J would be on the sport's biggest stage.

"He comes at you with those long, open strides, and you have a tendency to keep backing away from him because you think he's not really into his move yet. If you keep backing, if you fail to go up and challenge him, he'll simply glide right by you."—*Doug Moe, in a 1972* Sports Illustrated *story on Erving*

AND ONE!

"This is the best league that ever existed," he told Jim Murray of the *Los Angeles Times* in 1977. "Just look at the quality of ballplayers out of work, guys who can't crack this league. All the best talent in basketball is playing under one sign now."

He would reach great heights playing in the NBA. During his decade with the Philadelphia 76ers—in the merger, the Knicks *turned down* Erving's contract as a payment offer from the Nets, who were invading the team's territory, paving the way for him to join the Sixers—Erving would win an NBA title (1983), an MVP (1981), and would be an All-Star 11 times. If you coupled his five-year career in the ABA with his 11 years in the NBA, he would be sixth on the all-time scoring list with more than 30,000 points.

Art. **That, above all, is the other word people will tell you when you ask them about Julius Winfield Erving II.**

"For me, he is still the most exciting player who ever lived," the late Ralph Wiley wrote in a 1981 column in the *Oakland Tribune*. "He made the slam dunk a weapon and an art form."

Art. That, above all, is the other word people will tell you when you ask them about Julius Winfield Erving II. Remember that play we told you about? The one where, if you haven't seen it, you should ask? Well, here's a description of what happened: It's the fourth quarter of Game 4 of the 1980 NBA Finals. Lakers versus the Sixers. Erving catches a pass along the right side of the key. Abdul-Jabbar and teammate Mark Landsberger try to push Erving to the baseline and pin him there, forcing a turnover. What Erving does next is why he earned the nickname Dr. J.

He palms the ball in his right hand—it looks like a tennis ball—and leaps up underneath the right side of the backboard on the out-of-bounds side of the endline. With Abdul-Jabbar preventing him from coming back across, Erving decides to go up and under, extending that famously long arm on the *left side of the basket*. He flips the ball off the backboard, where it kisses the glass, and slides into the basket.

"I couldn't believe my eyes," said Magic Johnson, who witnessed the feat firsthand. "It's still the greatest move I've ever seen in a basketball game, the all-time greatest."

It's not hyperbole. Never was. Just ask anyone who has seen a clip of the Doctor in action.

Better yet, watch for yourself.

CHUCK TAYLOR ALL STARS

Basketball's First "Basketball Sneaker"

The simplicity is really what makes it.

Go ahead, marvel at the basic design. The inch-thick white, rubber sole at the bottom, with the thin black line running from toe to toe. The single piece of black or white canvas, with the two loop holes on the outside of the foot. The thick white laces from the feet all the way up to above the ankle, looking like perfectly made stripes. And then there's the capper: the circle rubber patch on the outside—right on the bump of the ankle bone—that tells you and everyone else, you're sporting the coolest, hippest sneaker ever invented: the *Chuck Taylor Converse All Star*.

NO. 37

"If you were going to play at the playground, the Chuck Taylor was *the* go-to shoe," said Ben Osborne, editor-in-chief of *SLAM* magazine and a basketball sneaker historian. "I think that was partly because it was cool and partly because—even years after it was intended to be that—it's the best basketball sneaker designed."

More than five decades before the Air Jordan by Nike revolutionized the way the basketball sneaker industry did business, there was the Chuck Taylor All Star by Converse, a simple offering by a rubber company that just so happened to make a sneaker and market it to athletes looking to get a better grip on the surfaces they were playing on. It was designed especially for the burgeoning sport known as basketball, played on hardwood and inside of tiny gyms with poor ventilation creating lots of slick surfaces.

If that's not improbable enough for you, consider that the man whose name is adorned on these 100-year-old kicks was a former hooper who began wearing the first iteration of

Someone's old Chucks.

the sneaker in high school, got a job as a salesman, and then proceeded to redesign it—giving it the iconic look it enjoys today and allowing it to become the unofficial sneaker of the serious basketball player for more than 30 years.

Bill Russell won all 11 of his NBA championships wearing Chuck Taylors.

"It's one of the most influential basketball shoes of all-time," Osborne said. "Part of that is because of what it became off the court. They didn't become a go-to staple for men, women, kids, the most comfortable shoe ever because Bill Russell wore them. It's not like Air Jordan, where one thing led to the other. It was really the best basketball shoe on the market for four decades—and really the only one that you could have, so guys wanted to wear them. And then, later on, became more of a pop cultural icon."

There's no way that Charles Hollis "Chuck" Taylor of Columbus, Indiana, could have ever imagined the empire that exists today because of the name that is now attached to the sneaker he loved.

When he went to Chicago, to Converse's offices to get a job as a salesman, it was predominantly because he liked and knew the product. He had started wearing the company's signature athletic sneaker in 1917 when it first hit the market. Taylor liked the feel and durability of the sneaker, but felt it needed more. A year after he was hired as a salesman, he suggested three changes to the existing shoe:

1. Change the design, to increase support of the ankle.

2. Reconfigure the sole for better traction.

3. Add a patch to the side.

Converse did both and, by 1932, put Taylor's name on the patch to signify his contributions to the sneaker and the brand. The shoe took off. With Taylor—who drove all over the country in a white Cadillac filled with sneakers in the trunk and keeping a locker in a Chicago warehouse but no permanent residence—hocking the sneaker, basketball players across the country went nuts for it. Taylor ran clinics, did demonstrations for high school and college programs. Since Taylor was a pretty good amateur player in his own right, players and coaches took him seriously.

The first US Olympic basketball team wore the sneakers in 1936. The first NCAA championship game in 1939 between Oregon and Ohio State featured players wearing Chuck Taylors. But the biggest break the sneaker ever got was when the National Basketball Association was formed in 1949. By the time television come along in the 1950s and games began being broadcast regionally and nationally, the Chuck Taylor was in the living room and on the sports pages for everyone to see.

"You can't overstate how dominant Chuck Taylors were," Bobbito Garcia, a sneaker enthusiast and pop culture expert told *Spin* in 2012. "Nike has something like 40 percent market share today. Through the 70s, Chuck Taylors had 70 or 80 percent market share for athletic shoes. For almost 50 years, there was very little competition for Converse. Nike, Adidas, Reebok—they didn't come up strong till the late 70s. It was basically Keds and Spalding and Converse. People wore what was available, which wasn't much."

Bill Russell won all 11 of his NBA championships wearing Chuck Taylors. On the night Wilt Chamberlain scored 100 points in a game, he did it wearing Chuck Taylors. Every time Julius Erving skied high for a dunk in his career, he did it in Chuck Taylors.

While seeing basketball superstars perform heroic exploits in Chucks on a daily basis helped their popularity, what gave the sneaker its credibility—especially as other shoemakers encroached on the territory in the 1960s and 70s—was that it was the sneaker of choice for the playground player.

"If you played street ball, you were going to wear Chuck Taylors," Osborne said. "That might've been influenced because you saw your favorite player wearing them, but if you were part of the *Heaven Is A Playground* (by Rick Telander) era, you were wearing Chucks."

The Chuck Taylor is still one of the most popular sneakers sold, but no longer synonymous with basketball. Its popularity is now based more in the worlds of fashion and music, and the counterculture. But the design remains virtually unchanged since Chuck Taylor made a few dynamic changes almost a century ago.

Simple sells.

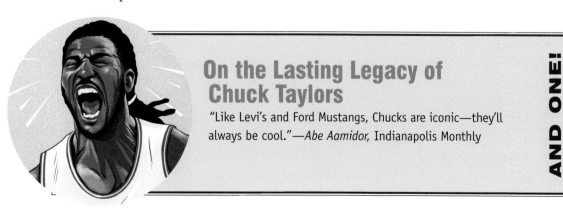

On the Lasting Legacy of Chuck Taylors

"Like Levi's and Ford Mustangs, Chucks are iconic—they'll always be cool."—*Abe Aamidor,* Indianapolis Monthly

AND ONE!

KOBE BRYANT TRADE

Lakers Find Their Next Superstar

As the lead-up to the 1996 NBA Draft intensified, it was clear that it would be a seminal night for the future of the league. The collection of franchises eager to reshape (and in some cases, redo) their directions was palpable. The NBA was still bringing the draft around to the various cities of its teams, and that year the draft would take place in the home of one of its most floundering franchises: Continental Airlines Arena— home of the New Jersey Nets.

The Nets had finished 30-52 during the 1995-96 season, the latest in a long string of failed seasons in East Rutherford. Another losing season meant the fourth straight year the team would be picking in the top-half of the draft.

There was a different feeling this time around, however. The talent level in the 1996 draft pool— especially at the top—was considered the best it had been in some time. Consensus No. 1 selection, Allen Iverson of Georgetown. College basketball's premier big man, Marcus Camby. Three dazzling two-guards: Stephon Marbury, Ray Allen, and Kerry Kittles. Small forwards Shareef Abdur-Rahim, Antoine Walker, and Samaki Walker (not related)— each of whom had a knack for scoring. Foreign talent (Vitaly Potapenko of Ukraine, Peja Stojakovic of Greece, and Steve Nash from Canada). A trio of big men with raw skill sets, but plenty of upside in Lorenzen Wright, Erick Dampier, and Todd Fuller. And then there were the two high school kids: a 6'11" swing-center named Jermaine O'Neal and a lithe shooting guard from the Philadelphia suburbs named Kobe Bryant.

In this July 12, 1996, file photo, Kobe Bryant, at age 17, holds his new Lakers jersey during a news conference.

It seemed as if there was no way a team looking to improve itself could miss on a prospect, which is why the Los Angeles Lakers were already hard at work trying to con someone out of their coveted draft position.

"He was special," then Lakers general manager Jerry West said during a press conference in 2016. "I'm surprised other people did not draft him. I'm really surprised because he was really special."

Throughout the charmed existence of the Lakers since their move to Los Angeles, the team has had the good fortune of having great things happen to it. In 1979, when the NBA decided who received the No. 1 pick by virtue of a coin toss between the teams with the worst two records in the conferences, the Lakers—who had dealt for the first-round selection of the New Orleans Jazz three years earlier—called tails. The Chicago Bulls called heads.

The Lakers won the toss and then selected Earvin "Magic" Johnson.

Three years later—*after winning the title*—the Lakers benefited from another previous shrewd move. Obtaining the first-round pick of the Cleveland Cavaliers, they won another coin toss, this time against the San Diego Clippers. The Clippers ended up with a fine player in Terry Cummings. The Lakers got a second future Hall of Famer to play alongside Magic and Kareem Abdul-Jabbar: James Worthy.

So when power-agent Arn Tellem—who represented the skinny 17-year-old Bryant—called his old friend West for advice, basketball history began lining up again for Los Angeles. Even with the success of Kevin Garnett the year prior, teams were still hesitant about drafting kids straight out of high school. But when they did, they were usually power forwards or centers. Guards making the jump from high school to the pros? Unheard of. So to test the draft waters for his client, Tellem arranged a workout with former Laker Michael Cooper.

"Obviously, the game has changed a lot. At one time big men were the people that everyone was looking for. Today, there are almost a dearth for big players that can play with their back to the basket. And Kobe kind of transcended some of the players we see today with the way he played the game and particularly with the enormous desire and toughness, never-quit attitude."—*Jerry West, talking about Kobe Bryant in 2016*

AND ONE!

Cooper was eight times a member of the league's all-defensive team during the 1980s. West had previously been in the "no-high schoolers" camp. The workout—where Bryant blew Cooper away—shocked him.

"The Lakers had no plans to work Kobe out," said former *Los Angeles Times* writer Mark Heisler. "Jerry West's eyes bugged out. And he starts telling people it was the greatest workout he had ever seen. Bill Fitch with the Clippers worked Kobe out during the same trip and he said the same thing. The Nets worked him out, too. Phoenix—which had the 15th pick—wanted him, too."

A little more than two weeks after the deal for Bryant was finalized, the Lakers signed prized free agent Shaquille O'Neal.

Word was out around the NBA. But how would it fall? There was a consensus, even after Bryant's stellar workouts, that he wouldn't go any earlier than No. 8 to the Nets. (The Celtics at No. 6 loved Bryant, but felt he still needed polishing. The Clippers at No. 7 did as well, but were in the market for a center.) The problem lay within the conscience of the Nets' new head coach—and general manager—John Calipari.

Hired straight from college, Calipari told confidants how much he loved Bryant and his game. *But*, he was a high school kid and the Nets couldn't necessarily afford to wait around for development. Worse: Bryant was already making overtures that if the Nets drafted him, he would go and play in Europe—something the perennial losers could ill afford.

"He said he wasn't going to play there," recalled Peter Vecsey, longtime NBA writer for the *New York Post* and a member of TNT's broadcast crew on that draft night. "But I knew that was a smokescreen. Where was he going to go? He was coming straight out of high school—he wanted to play in the NBA. He was going to play for the Nets, they just had to take him."

Calipari and New Jersey couldn't do it. They took Kittles instead.

As this was unfolding, West was stealthily trying to move up on the draft board, while Bryant slowly slipped down it. He finally found a buyer—the Charlotte Hornets, who would draft Bryant and then send him to Los Angeles in exchange for center Vlade Divac.

"Kobe was kind of a last minute thing for them," said Heisler. "They weren't thinking about him until that workout kind of fell into their laps. But, the piece fit perfectly, because they could get him for Vlade."

It was another stroke of genius by West and the Lakers. A little more than two weeks after the deal for Bryant was finalized, the Lakers signed prized free agent Shaquille O'Neal. Four seasons later, the duo would lead Los Angeles to its first of three straight titles. Bryant would then win two more without O'Neal, cementing his legacy among the sport's elite.

Not bad for an impromptu workout.

HIGH SCHOOLERS IN THE NBA

How Early Is Too Early and How Ready Do You Have to Be?

NO. 39

At the 2016 NBA Draft, the Milwaukee Bucks made a small—but somewhat important—contribution to the history of the league. Holding the 10th overall pick in the first round, the Bucks decided to take a 7'1", 216-pound Australian named Thon Maker. Not a huge deal on its face, right? Maker was tall, athletic, and possessed a game that scouts felt was just scratching the surface. Here's the catch: Thon Maker was 19 years old and had not played at a level above his senior year of high school, thus making him the first high-school-to-the-NBA draft choice to be taken in the first round in a decade.

Maker exploited a loophole in the existing NBA collective bargaining agreement that declared any player wishing to enter the draft had to be at least 19 years old and be one year removed from his graduation from high school. Maker, who was born in Sudan, but made his way to American schools by way of Australia, graduated high school in Virginia in June of 2015, but then stashed himself at a prep school in Ontario, Canada, for a year. Then, despite being pursued by some of the top college programs, he announced he was turning pro.

In effect, he entered the NBA through the back door, precisely what the league was hoping to avoid when it changed a long-standing rule after the 2005 draft.

Minnesota Timberwolves rookie Kevin Garnett, who jumped from high school to the NBA, having some fun for official photos during media day on October 5, 1995.

SHORT LIST

High Schoolers Taken in Top Five of NBA Draft

Year	Player	Pick	Team
1975	Darryl Dawkins	5th	Philadelphia 76ers
1995	Kevin Garnett	5th	Minnesota Timberwolves
1999	Jonathan Bender	5th	Indiana Pacers
2000	Darius Miles	3rd	Los Angeles Clippers
2001	Kwame Brown	1st	Washington Wizards
2001	Tyson Chandler	2nd	Los Angeles Clippers
2001	Eddy Curry	4th	Chicago Bulls
2003	LeBron James	1st	Cleveland Cavaliers
2004	Dwight Howard	1st	Orlando Magic
2004	Shaun Livingston	4th	Los Angeles Clippers

He is not the first player to take advantage of the loophole—Brandon Jennings and Emmanuel Mudiay graduated high school and played professionally overseas for a year—but the last first-round pick who last played basketball in high school was Gerald Green in 2005.

After Kevin Garnett, the *USA Today* player of the year, bypassed college and went straight to the NBA (he was the No. 5 pick in 1995)—and was an immediate success—the floodgates opened. From 1995 to 2005, a total of 39 players made the jump from high school to the pros. Some were hits (Garnett, Kobe Bryant, Jermaine O'Neal, LeBron James, Dwight Howard), while others (Darius Miles, Eddy Curry, DeSagana Diop, Robert Swift) were not.

Before Garnett's glass-ceiling shattering debut, high schoolers in the NBA was a foreign concept—only three had ever done it from 1947 all the way up to 1994, and just one (Darryl Dawkins) was picked in the first round. High schoolers were seen as too immature, both mentally and physically, to compete nightly in the pros. But after Garnett's success, NBA general managers did what NBA general managers do: They tried to copycat the process.

Out were the traditional buckets that NBA prospects had their skills grouped by—"size, speed, ability"—and in came new ones. Players were measured by "wingspan" and were less evaluated and more projected. It was a modern day gold rush, with speculators all over the country peeking in dark corners to see if the next great NBA player was there hiding. Players quickly started becoming evaluated earlier and earlier. Player rankings were no longer relegated to seniors and rising juniors, but now for sophomores and freshmen, and *eighth-graders*. Much like the explosion of taking European players around the same time, it seemed that every NBA team had to have a high school talent.

The bubble grew and grew, all while teams continued to reach further and further to draft marginal talent who had been given bad advice. The bubble burst in 2001—high school players made up three of the first four picks in the draft. And while Kwame Brown (No. 1) and Eddy Curry (No. 4) had sustained NBA careers, only Tyson Chandler (No. 2) ever made an All-Star Game or won a championship. In 2003, Ndudi Ebi—who was picked No. 26 in the first round—played two seasons. James Lang, a second-round pick that year, would only ever play 11 games in the NBA.

NBA teams needed to be saved from themselves.

"It's there to protect them," Jonathan Abrams, author of *Boys Among Men*, a book about the preps-to-pros movement, told *The Atlantic* in 2016. "So that they're able to see these guys when they're more mature and project where they were good."

Players have argued that not being able to declare for the draft hurts their earning power, as college sports still does not pay its athletes.

In 2005, the NBA outlawed high school players jumping to the league. The rule was as much designed to protect the quality of the NBA product as it was to allow players to get a chance to develop their games in college for a year (or longer) instead of being burned by bad decisions. To prevent cautionary tales, such as Lenny Cooke—who was once the No. 1 player in the country before being dethroned by James—turning pro in 2002. Cooke went undrafted, but the closest he came to playing in the NBA was a short stint with the Celtics' summer league team.

Players have argued that not being able to declare for the draft hurts their earning power, as college sports still does not pay its athletes. But Derrick Rose, Blake Griffin, John Wall, Kyrie Irving, Anthony Davis, Andrew Wiggins, and Karl-Anthony Towns are all No. 1 picks who have become stars in the NBA, while spending at least one year in college. Thon Maker's selection as a top-10 pick while not seeing the inside of a college classroom may change all that. It may not.

There will be other players and other loopholes to exploit, regardless of whether or not the NBA changes the rule going forward, though there is little doubt that stemming the tide of players each spring jumping from high school gyms to NBA arenas has saved the careers of numerous kids. All it takes is one person giving bad advice to ruin the career of a player. Once the decision is made there is no turning back.

In 1998, Korleone Young was a 6'7" kid with a huge upside coming out of high school. A couple of years in college and he could have been a high draft pick. He came out early, completely unexpectedly. He was drafted in the second round by the Detroit Pistons.

His stint in the NBA lasted 15 minutes.

WNBA
They Finally Got Next

It started as an idea to replicate what the men had done.

In the summer of 1994, NBA commissioner David Stern and his No. 2, Russ Granik, had been toying around with the idea of taking the excitement surrounding the league and duplicating it with women players. After all, they saw what was happening in the women's game in college and could tell there was a definite interest. But how do you get the college popularity to translate into the pros—when there wasn't even a league?

Enter Val Ackerman.

She had been a liaison for the NBA and USA Basketball, where she had been on the board of directors since 1990. During that time, Ackerman had been a part of the creation of the 1992 Men's national team— "The Dream Team"—that had captivated the world during the Barcelona Summer Olympics. After seeing the success of the men's Dream Team, Ackerman and others began to kick around the idea of doing the same thing for the women's national team. Take the best women's players from college and playing elsewhere to create a Women's Dream Team.

She also knew that the NBA had interest in creating a women's pro basketball league and saw the mutual benefit each aim could have on the other.

"In 1994, we were kind of reeling competitively," Ackerman recalled. "But we knew that David was keeping his eye on potentially a pro league. So, in 1995, USA Basketball became our way of getting from what was happening in women's college basketball to the pros. It was kind of our nexus."

Knowing the 1996 Summer Olympics—being held in Atlanta—was a year away, Ackerman helped form the Women's Dream Team a year early. She went to Stern and Granik with this idea: Form the team, let them tour around the country for a year, and test the waters

NO. 40

WNBA players Nicky Anosike and Courtney Vandersloot.

SHORT LIST

Most WNBA Championships

Franchise	Titles	Years
Houston Comets	4	1997, 1998, 1999, 2000
Detroit Shock	3	2003, 2006, 2008
Phoenix Mercury	3	2007, 2009, 2014
Minnesota Lynx	3	2011, 2013, 2015
Los Angeles Sparks	3	2001, 2002, 2016
Seattle Storm	2	2004, 2010

that way. It was a no-lose situation. USA Basketball ran everything, while the NBA watched to see if it would work.

The roster was a who's who of the best women's players the United States had to offer: Dawn Staley, Sheryl Swoopes, Lisa Leslie, Nikki McCray—and the star of stars: Rebecca Lobo, fresh off of a four-year run at Connecticut where the Huskies had captivated the country with a 35-0 run to win the national championship. Lobo, despite being one of the youngest players on the team, was quickly its biggest attraction.

"She was a rookie on that team," Ackerman said. "She graduated in '95. But this team also had Sheryl Swoopes, Lisa Leslie, Dawn Staley—the very best veteran women's players of that time. They were the ones that were starting and starring. But given what UConn was doing and what Rebecca had accomplished, it was unimaginable to have a team like that without her on it."

The tour was a success. The Summer Olympics the following year would only compound that, as the United States won the gold medal for the first time since 1988.

But the NBA already had its answer.

"That pre-Olympics tour and those games convinced us that a time was right for a women's pro league," Ackerman said.

Just shy of four months before the United States won the gold medal in Atlanta, on April 24, 1996, the NBA called a press conference in New York City to announce the creation of the WNBA. Three players from that USA Basketball team—Leslie, Swoopes, and Lobo—were chosen to be the new faces of the league.

With the full backing of the league and its board of governors, the WNBA would begin in the summer of 1997 in eight cities: New York, Cleveland, Charlotte, and Houston in the Eastern Conference; and Los Angeles, Phoenix, Sacramento, and Utah in the Western Conference.

Under the slogan, "We Got Next"—created by 29-year-old Manhattan advertising copywriter Amie Murstein—the league officially tipped off on June 21, 1997. The WNBA enjoyed everything that its male NBA counterpart did: the use of arenas, access to the same fan bases, and most importantly, the television deals. Marquee games were shown on NBC, while the league also struck deals with ESPN and Lifetime Television to carry games.

"It changed the way people perceived women's basketball," Lobo said. "It completely changed girls and their interest in sports. Parents were now making sure that their kids are involved in these opportunities. I live in a small town now and there's a ton of girls who play basketball."

By 2000, the WNBA would double in size. Franchises were added in Detroit and Washington in 1998; Orlando and Minnesota in 1999; Indiana, Seattle, Miami, and Portland in 2000. Lobo, Swoopes, and Leslie delivered as advertised, becoming the pillars the league was built on as they guided their teams to championship runs.

Swoopes—along with Tina Thompson and Cynthia Cooper—created the league's first dynasty with the Houston Comets, winning the first four WNBA titles. In 2000, President Bill Clinton invited the team to the White House—the first time a women's sports team had been invited to an audience with the president.

Since then, the league has undergone expansion and contraction like any other pro sports league. Only three of the original teams remain in their original cities (New York, Phoenix, and Los Angeles), while four other franchises formed after that inaugural season folded. But the league

In 2000, President Bill Clinton invited the team to the White House—the first time a women's sports team had been invited to an audience with the president.

is still strong as it finishes its 20th season: There are 12 franchises, with new and exciting players continuing the legacy that was begun two decades earlier.

It all began with Ackerman being able to connect the dots between what she knew at USA Basketball and what the NBA wanted to find out. There was an audience for women's basketball—it just had to be done with the right players and in the right markets. The barnstorming tour that the future Olympic team went on proved that to an unsure NBA. So when the league was officially created, Stern beamed as he announced its first president: Val Ackerman.

THE WHITE SHADOW

A Simple Premise for a Complicated Time

When the news began to trickle out in late March of 2016, the tributes began pouring in from every corner. Sports figures and actors. Politicians and newsmakers. Celebrities and writers. They were mourning the passing of Ken Howard, a distinguished character actor who won a Tony Award and two Emmy Awards during a career spanning the better part of six decades.

At 71, Howard's passing was sad, but what it—what *he*—represented was so much more. For a large generation of American television watchers, Ken Howard was the authority figure the country was looking for, the one it needed to bridge the gap between social, economic, and most importantly, racial classes.

All because Howard's portrayal of an ex–pro basketball player who returns to the roots of the game at its purest form—high school—resonated with so many.

The premise of *The White Shadow* was this: Ken Reeves, an aging, broken-down NBA player with the Chicago Bulls suffers a career-ending back injury. He is asked to become the head coach at Carver High School in South Central Los Angeles—a white man, coaching players who were primarily black and Hispanic. It was a concept so foreign that the network that eventually aired the show, CBS, originally wanted it to be a sitcom.

Old white coach. Young black kids. A barrel of laughs!

Except Howard—who would later serve as the president of the Screen Actors Guild—and the show's creator, Bruce Paltrow, wouldn't budge. They wanted the program to be an hour-long drama when it debuted in November 1978. More importantly than that, they

The coach and his team from *The White Shadow*.

wanted to tackle issues that were plaguing everyday Americans. CBS relented and *The White Shadow* was born.

"I think the reason it endures is because it wasn't really like other shows," Howard told the *Sporting News* during an interview in 2005. "It was a homemade idea. It did not come through traditional television channels. I went to Bruce Paltrow with the idea, we went to CBS, and they bought it. So there was a uniqueness that still resonates today. The shorts were a lot shorter, of course, but the themes and the humor resonate."

When Howard died of an undisclosed illness, it brought in tributes from all corners of the world . . .

The White Shadow left no social stone unturned. There were episodes dealing with drugs, alcohol, homosexuality, sexually transmitted diseases, child abuse, and disabilities. The audience never felt coddled or failed to receive the full picture. This was a snapshot of life in America's inner cities at the end of the 1970s and early 1980s, when youth culture was undergoing a seismic shift.

Instead of ignoring the issues young adults were going through—or patronizing them through the words written by out-of-touch scriptwriters—*The White Shadow* brought them out into the open. Made them easier to talk about. Put a human face to problems that suburban America thought it could easily ignore.

"As an only child watching way too much television at the time, I was patiently awaiting my own show, the one that spoke to me and only me," sportswriter Bill Simmons wrote on ESPN.com after Paltrow's death in 2002. "I love 'The Brady Bunch,' 'Gilligan's Island,' all the aforementioned sitcoms, 'Charlie's Angels,' 'Three's Company,' 'The Incredible Hulk' . . . but this was different. It felt like they created 'The White Shadow' just for me." And Simmons was a white kid from suburban Boston.

What made the show so appealing and so resonating was that it didn't patronize its viewers. In a time when television stereotyped minorities as badly as society did, writers and producers of *The White Shadow* didn't set the bar low. More often than not, black actors were relegated to the pimps, street criminals, and drug dealers on television, if there were no roles for the butler or token comedic relief. Hispanic actors were in the same boat. Not on the set as members of Carver High's varsity basketball team.

Part of the appeal, was the flawed character of Reeves—modeled after his high school coach growing up on Long Island. Howard's portrayal of the juxtaposed ex-player-turned-coach to kids he didn't easily identify with broke down any barriers that the audience may have had. Reeves' plight was humane, but as he learned, so too, did viewers.

"Well, I didn't want him to be ideal," Howard said. "He wound up being that, but that was never how he was supposed to be. He was a journeyman NBA player before the knee injury, and he was supposed to be flawed. He wasn't supposed to be perfect. I think those people make the best coaches, the imperfect ones. It's like Jerry West used to say, about having trouble coaching because he was such a perfectionist as a player, and such a great player, that it is hard for him to be a coach—you can't understand why your players can't just do what you did. So, the Shadow was supposed to be flawed. It made him a better teacher. He was not supposed to be a great white knight, which, at the end of the show, he seemed to become."

The White Shadow only lasted three seasons. By the end, CBS caved to pressure and tried to make the show more mainstream—guest stars regularly dropped by and the tone of the show changed. It became more positive, focusing less on the character-driven storylines that had helped win acclaim from fans.

It would find an endearing home in the hearts of many through reruns and home releases, allowing those who grew up with the show to relive what made it so transcendent. When Howard died of an undisclosed illness, it brought in tributes from all corners of the world— foreign syndication gave the show legions of fans. No tribute captured the show's impact more than in Turkey. Upon Howard's death, members of the Turkish Basketball Federation began a movement to name an arena after Howard.

And if you think that sounds bizarre, well, watch an episode or two.

"*The White Shadow* tackled a lot of challenging issues in American society, and showed the difference a coach, and basketball more generally, can make in young people's lives," Turkish Basketball Federation CEO Hedo Turkoglu said. "The lessons about life you learn on the basketball court don't recognize borders, and I think that's one of the reasons the show was so popular in Turkey."

"It's impossible to describe how much Ken Howard as Ken Reeves meant to 12-year-old me. I'm going to run some laps in his memory. Godspeed."

—*Mike Vaccaro of the* New York Post *on Twitter after Howard's death in 2016*

AND ONE!

NBA EXPANSION
The Footprint Finally Expands

The rumors. That's what Pat Williams still remembers. Going down to the lobby of the Arizona Biltmore Hotel every morning at the 1986 NBA Board of Governors meetings, milling about, chit-chatting with different NBA officials. Every conversation—no, every interaction—with someone different became another exercise in trying to shake loose the truth.

Did you hear they're just going to take Charlotte?

Did you hear they're only going to take one team from Florida?

Did you hear they're not taking Minnesota?

Did you hear they're not going to take any of us?

"We honestly thought they would take just one of us—maybe two," Williams said. "The rumors. They were flying every day. On and on and on went the rumors."

The league had been seriously weighing the prospect of expanding its ranks for the first time since adding the Dallas Mavericks in 1980. Williams was a part of the group lobbying to bring a franchise to Orlando, Florida. He had been a general manager in Chicago, Atlanta, and Philadelphia, where he helped build the 1983 NBA champion 76ers. But here he was, part of a group trying to convince the NBA to come to a minor city in central Florida with fewer than a million residents.

He wasn't alone.

There was a cadre of groups all angling to get a piece of the NBA pie. After years when the league couldn't get any interest in adding more franchises—in fact, in the early

Charlotte Hornets forward Kelly Tripucka models Alexander Julian's new travel uniform for the NBA expansion team on July 20, 1988.

NBA Expansion Franchises (since 1980)

Franchise	Year Began
Miami Heat	1988
Charlotte Hornets	1988
Minnesota Timberwolves	1989
Orlando Magic	1989
Vancouver Grizzlies	1995
Toronto Raptors	1995
Charlotte Bobcats	2004

1980s after the addition of Dallas, some thought the league should *contract*—business picked up. Behind the revolution of Magic Johnson, Larry Bird, and the burgeoning talent of Michael Jordan, interest was renewed in trying to join the NBA.

While there were nearly a dozen cities with some form of ownership group in place and ready to go, the consensus was that four cities stood the best chance to be selected: Minneapolis, Charlotte, Miami, and Orlando. So when the prospective franchises were invited to make their 30-minute pitches to the league's Board of Governors in Phoenix that year, no one knew what would happen.

"It wasn't until the owners meetings the following April that the shocking news came—they would be taking all four of us," Williams, now the senior vice president of the Orlando Magic recalled. "But the price tag was $32.5 million—up $7 million from what we were told in October. There was one stipulation though: they weren't taking all four of us at once."

The NBA had decided to expand—but would do it in shifts. In 1988, the Miami Heat and Charlotte Hornets would enter the league. The next season, the Magic and Minnesota Timberwolves would join. Unbeknownst to the competing ownership groups at the time, the league also had its eyes on expanding beyond the four new teams.

They had their eyes on Canada, where the Toronto Raptors and Vancouver Grizzlies would join in 1995. "This is international expansion in a most comfortable way," David Stern, the former NBA commissioner told the *Toronto Star* in 1993. "It's a safe step out and a compelling one because of the size of the market and the likelihood of success."

The decision to expand from 24 teams in 1980 to 30 teams by 1995 was a calculated one. In most cases, the NBA teams that joined were the only sports show in town. They brought the NBA into different markets that hadn't had basketball and opened the doors for fans to catch a Jordan, a Barkley, a Ewing on a nightly basis. At a time when the NBA was booming, more people got in on the action.

And in many ways, the additions of NBA franchises helped build the cities around them.

"Orlando in 1986, 1987—there really wasn't much of a downtown at all," Williams remembered. "There was really no airport, no convention center. There was no Universal Studios. No

Disney Animal Kingdom. No movie studios or theme parks. There was just Walt Disney World. But we kept saying to the league, 'Evaluate us in 10 years, 20 years, 30 years—please.' What has happened in this community is absolutely breathtaking."

Ditto for the likes of Charlotte and Minneapolis. And Miami became a town known for something other than its football.

"The way Charlotte has grown exponentially is unbelievable," Tim Kempton, a center on the Hornets' inaugural season team, told *Charlotte Magazine* in 2013. "It was a banking hub, but it was still a small, southeastern city with not a lot of growth to it yet, but you could see it coming. Every time I go back, there are still people who come up and say hello to me. . . . It legitimized Charlotte. 'We're here. Look at us over in the southeast of America.' That led to the (NFL's Carolina) Panthers coming here. Do they put the Panthers there if the Charlotte Hornets don't work? Who knows."

It hasn't been all roses, though. The Hornets defected to New Orleans in 2002, leaving behind a trail of bitterness through owner George Shinn. The Timberwolves have only made the playoffs eight times in their history. The Magic have made the NBA Finals twice, while the Heat are the only team from that group to have won a title—winning three. The Vancouver Grizzlies ditched Canada after six years, relocating to Memphis. Toronto remains, but has never enjoyed sustained success.

Still, the Class of 1988-89 in many ways changed the way the NBA operated. Because the franchises were starting from the ground floor, they weren't very good early on—earning them years of high draft picks. That opened the door for tandems of talented players, who complemented the established stars around the league. Miami landed Glen Rice and Steve Smith; Charlotte had Larry Johnson and Muggsy Bogues; Orlando had Shaquille O'Neal and Penny Hardaway; Minnesota had Kevin Garnett and Stephon Marbury.

. . . the Class of 1988-89 in many ways changed the way the NBA operated.

All of those great players took the floor nightly for their new, proud cities. And suddenly fans in New York and Chicago and Los Angeles began to get excited when the Hornets and Magic and Heat and Timberwolves came to town.

Not bad for four cities just hoping for a shot to join the fun.

"It took the NBA deep into the south," Williams said. "It filled that Carolina market and then opened up Florida, with its huge population base in a way that had never occurred before. That has brought nothing but plusses to the NBA. So we're now a league that has a deep toe-hold in the south. And that's been a great plus."

NBA GOES TO ASIA

Basketball Finally Comes to the Planet's Largest Population

June 26, 2002.

The Theater at Madison Square Garden was full. It always was. This was the NBA Draft—a once-afterthought in the minds of the league that had become a full-on spectacle every late June. It was a strange time though for the league. Transitional, even. Michael Jordan had been retired (for a second time) since 1998. Kobe Bryant and Shaquille O'Neal had formed the league's premier duo in Los Angeles, catapulting the Lakers back to prominence. But the NBA was still searching for an identity to pin itself to as the new millennium began.

One year earlier, the NBA had gathered in the same building on a similar warm June night to select its next bumper crop of superstars. The 2001 draft, though, went over as smoothly as a glass of scalding hot water: Kwame Brown—the first high schooler taken No. 1 overall—led a cadre of kids who bypassed college and went right into the arms of NBA teams salivating over their potential talent. Of the first 10 picks in 2001, one was a foreigner, four were high schoolers, and four were college players who were freshmen or sophomores. Only one—Duke's Shane Battier—was a senior.

So, when the 2002 NBA Draft approached the witching hour, there was a sense that it could be the draft night that shaped the way the NBA did business for the next decade-plus. The reason why was a 21-year-old, 7'5", 296-pound gentle giant from a place where basketball players were still a mystery.

Yao Ming, who was inducted into the
Basketball Hall of Fame in 2016.

But in the minds of the league, Yao Ming would be the key to the future of the game.

"The pressure on him, some sensed that he was the ambassador for this entire country," former NBA commissioner David Stern told a panel at the Brookings Institute in 2014. "And all of a sudden, Americans were going to learn more about China than they knew in other ways, through Yao Ming. And he took that responsibility. And in an interesting way, through television, our Chinese fans were going to learn more about America through Yao Ming."

For over a decade, the NBA had been looking for a way to break into the Asian market. Basketball, through the exploits of Magic Johnson and Larry Bird in the 1980s, was gaining globally. That decade led to more European players in the league. Michael Jordan and the Dream Team at the 1992 Olympics created an even bigger boom—suddenly players from all parts of the world saw the NBA as a realistic destination. The Far East countries still seemed to be on the outskirts. Stern and the NBA wanted to change that.

Yao was the perfect piece to complete the puzzle the NBA had been trying to solve since the early 1990s.

For starters, China's population topped a billion people in the early 1980s and continued to climb as the 1990s began. From a bodies standpoint, there was plenty of opportunity. In addition, despite the stranglehold that communism had on the country, it was beginning to become more and more Americanized. McDonald's were popping up. American hotel companies had a foothold. It was less and less a mysterious world power and more and more a familiar face, with different rules. The NBA first put an employee on the ground in China—a senior vice president named Rob Levine—in 1990. The idea behind Levine's presence was to help cultivate an interest in and market for basketball and the NBA.

"We're not introducing the game to them," Levine told the *New York Times* in 2008. "We're introducing our game."

Basketball was already popular in China, but the population was not ingrained in NBA culture like the Europeans or even South Americans were. Slowly but surely, having Levine on the front lines in China began to pay off. Players began regularly going there to conduct clinics and by the late 1990s began taking goodwill trips to China, Taiwan, and Japan. In 1994, CCTV-China broadcast the first game of the NBA Finals—*live*—marking the first time it had been done in the country's history.

The game was booming on the other side of the globe, but Asian fans had yet to find a touchpoint in the NBA they could grab on to. That came when the Chinese Basketball Association finally announced that its most marketable star—Yao—would be eligible to be drafted into the NBA.

"Our guys in the U.S. didn't believe that there was a Chinese kid that tall," Terry Rhoads, Nike's director of marketing for China told *ESPN The Magazine* in a 2000 story on Yao. "Once we convinced them, they invited us to bring him to a Nike camp in Paris that summer. . . . Del Harris, then the Lakers coach, was at the camp and he fell in love with Yao. He was telling everybody, 'I gotta get a picture with that kid because one day he's gonna have a real impact in the NBA.'"

Yao was the perfect piece to complete the puzzle the NBA had been trying to solve since the early 1990s. He wasn't just a sideshow; he was good. Witness his eight career All-Star selections during a seven-year career that was cut short by nagging injuries. Or that he was inducted into the National Basketball Hall of Fame in 2016. During his time with the Houston Rockets, Yao was one of the most popular players in the league.

It allowed the NBA to unlock the Asian market in the biggest and best way possible. The league and its players have continued to make trips to China, Taiwan, Japan, and South Korea. To begin the 2016-17 season, the Rockets and New Orleans Pelicans played two preseason games in China—one in Shanghai and another in Beijing.

"We are thrilled to bring NBA teams once again to Beijing and Shanghai," NBA commissioner Adam Silver said when he announced the two games would be played in China. "NBA fans in China are incredibly passionate and knowledgeable about the game of basketball. The China Games deliver the live, authentic NBA experience to our Chinese fans and provide our teams and players an opportunity to learn more about the Chinese people and culture."

A truly foreign concept more than two decades earlier.

On the Global Impact Yao Ming Had on the NBA

"Nobody was that important; nobody embraced the universal game; nobody was as important to Asia entering the NBA conversation as Yao Ming."—*Jack McCallum,* Sports Illustrated

AND ONE!

MIKE KRZYZEWSKI

One Letter Becomes Synonymous with Success

44

On the afternoon of the latest in what has been a long, long line of successful days, Mike Krzyzewski was just trying to blend in and not make a fuss. It was a cold January Sunday in 2015 at the world's most famous arena, Madison Square Garden, after the Duke head coach had captured win No. 1,000. Krzyzewski was being lauded by players—past and present—family members, friends, fans, well-wishers, and lookers-on. As always he was the center of attention, the star of the hour, the center of the universe.

He would, just a few short months later, win his fourth national championship.

He has, as of the start of the 2016-17 college basketball season, 1,043 wins—most in Division 1 history. Only two college coaches—men's or women's, across any level collegiately—have more than the head coach of the Duke Blue Devils. That's before you bring up the lifetime contract he now has at the school where the court he coaches on *already* bears his name. Before you realize that his program has produced more No. 1 picks in the NBA Draft than any other school. Before you realize that before he arrived in Durham, North Carolina, Duke had been to four Final Fours in its history—and since has been to *12*.

Or being a member of both the Basketball Hall of Fame and College Basketball Hall of Fame by the age of 60. The two Olympic gold medals as head coach, two as an assistant and two FIBA world championships. The career resume of Krzyzewski is long and distinguished, but way back when—when winning didn't come easy and recruits chose other schools instead of his—he was just another coach on the chopping block.

Duke University head coach Mike Krzyzewski during a timeout on January 12, 2012.

"Durham was not a pleasant place to be in 1983," ESPN analyst and former Duke star Jay Bilas told YahooSports.com in 2015. "There was a lot of discontentment around the program, and it was vocal. Heck, there was a petition circling around calling for Mike to be fired. I saw it. One of the Iron Dukes [Duke boosters] showed it to me, which I thought was kind of a classless move. But there were a lot of people who were really unhappy."

When Duke hired the little-known Krzyzewski after five relatively pedestrian seasons at Army, he seemed like an odd choice. He was Polish through-and-through, hailing from Chicago, before spending his college years at West Point, where he played for Bobby Knight. After returning from active duty, Krzyzewski took a job with his former coach for a season at Indiana. Then, it was off to be the head coach at Army.

Duke had been a basketball power in the 1960s under Vic Bubas, making the NCAA Tournament four times, with two third-place finishes and a national runner-up finish in 1964. But when Bubas retired, Duke's successes faded. After Bucky Waters and Neill McGeachy had their turns coaching the Blue Devils, Bill Foster showed up in 1974. Foster had a reputation as a program-builder, and quickly began building the foundation Krzyzewski's success would be built on when he took over in 1980.

"When (Krzyzewski) recruited that famous [Johnny] Dawkins class, it was only five years removed from us going to the Final Four," said Johnny Moore, Duke's former sports information director during the Foster era and early Krzyzewski years. "Kids had seen that you could be successful at Duke."

He made the NIT quarterfinals his first season, but had losing campaigns the next two years. Fans began to wonder if the job was too big for him. By 1985-86, they had their answer as Duke made it to the national championship game, losing to Louisville.

"To do it here, to win the 1,000th (at Madison Square Garden), you've got to be a lucky guy. I like my place, Cameron, but this is a magical place."—*Mike Krzyzewski, after capturing his 1,000th career win in 2015*

AND ONE!

The rest, as they say, is history.

As the wins continued to pile up, the NCAA Tournament appearances mounted, and the recruits and fans never stopped lining up behind him. Through nearly four decades as the head coach of the Blue Devils, Krzyzewski has built himself into an empire. He has shunned the NBA, while retaining relationships with some of the game's greatest players—virtually none of whom played for him. He has become identified as the personification of winning, coaching Duke to multiple titles and USA Basketball to two Olympic golds. That's led to lucrative endorsement deals with American Express and Chevrolet.

He took something with the beginnings of a foundation, but decided to build the house himself.

None of that would have been possible without the wins on the court in Cameron Indoor Stadium—and elsewhere.

"It's a remarkable accomplishment to win as many games as Mike has as a coach," Knight said following Krzyzewski's 1,000th win. "However, being able to coach as well as he has for as many years as he has, is even more remarkable."

Amazingly Krzyzewski shows no signs of slowing down. Those around him say he's just as invested and involved in the Duke program as when he started. As the recruiting game has intensified and players have more say in where they want to play, Krzyzewski has adapted. For years, he would only recruit kids who would likely stay all four years—now he has morphed that to adjust to the age of the one-and-done player. No matter. He's still racking up Ws.

"When you have believers, you're happy all the time," Krzyzewski told ESPN.com after winning his fourth national championship in 2015. "My wife would tell you that. When you can be creative instead of trying to figure out attitudes, it's so much easier. I never had to figure it out. When you get kids like I have, it's so easy."

It is now, but it wasn't at first. Perhaps that's what makes the legend of the man with the hard-to-pronounce last name all the more magical. He wasn't gifted a great situation or handed the keys to a great car and asked not to wreck it. He took something with the beginnings of a foundation, but decided to build the house himself.

And in the process, everyone forgot the name they struggled to say and simply went with a much easier moniker: Coach K.

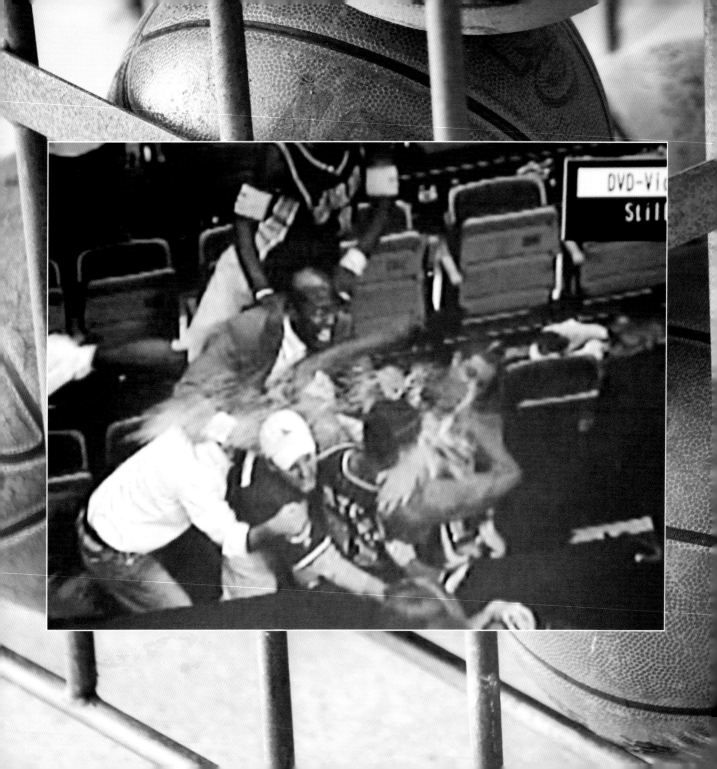

"MALICE AT THE PALACE"

The NBA Gives Itself the Blackest Eye Yet

It doesn't matter how you watched it—live, on *SportsCenter* the next morning, the local news, or on YouTube years later. The first visual clips of the "Malice at the Palace" are jarring even today: Professional athletes in the stands fighting and punching fans; fans on the court, fighting and punching professional athletes. Even in this day and age where every misstep—big and small—is documented, replayed, and dissected, it's still hard to fathom what happened on the night of November 19, 2004, during a game between the Indiana Pacers and the Detroit Pistons.

The cauldron of emotion had been bubbling since the previous season. The Pacers—winners of 61 games and the best record in the NBA—had been eliminated in six games by the underdog Pistons, in a series that was hotly contested. Indiana, believing it had the better team, stewed all summer waiting for a chance to play Detroit again.

And perhaps exact a pound of flesh—and maybe a sense of retribution from what was lost the season before.

"We did not like each other," Pacers center Jermaine O'Neal recalled to *Grantland* in a 2014 oral history of the game. "It was one of those old-school Knicks-Bulls rivalries I used to always see on TV and see the guys getting into it, little pushes and stuff like that. That's how we viewed it."

Video framegrab showing spectator John Green, center with baseball cap, holding the Indiana Pacers's Ron Artest during a fight between fans and several Indiana players on November 19, 2004.

SHORT LIST

Malice at the Palace Punishments

Player	Team	NBA Suspension	Salary Lost
Ron Artest	Pacers	86 games	$4,995,000
Stephen Jackson	Pacers	30 games	$1,700,000
Jermaine O'Neal	Pacers	15 games	$4,111,000
Ben Wallace	Pistons	6 games	$400,000
Anthony Johnson	Pacers	5 games	$122,222
Reggie Miller	Pacers	1 game	$61,111
Chauncey Billups	Pistons	1 game	$60,611
Derrick Coleman	Pistons	1 game	$50,000
Elden Campbell	Pistons	1 game	$48,888

So when the two teams met just a little over two weeks into the 2004-05 season, it was considered must-see-TV. ESPN, which was in its third season as the league's television partner, put the game in its primetime slot on Friday night—showcasing it for the nation. And for much of the game, it lived up to the billing. The Pacers and Pistons went at it on the court, with Indiana taking an 80–66 lead into the fourth quarter on the road. At that time, the Pistons' home court—The Palace of Auburn Hills—was considered one of the toughest road environments in the league, so as the defending champions tried to come back against their rivals, the building's energy was ratcheted up.

But as the Pistons fell further and further behind, and the comeback attempt looked more in vain, things on the court began to spiral out of control. Fouls became more aggressive and more physical. With 1:25 remaining in a game where the Pacers held a double-digit lead, Pistons center Ben Wallace slammed into Pacer forward Ron Artest hard, knocking him into the basket support. No foul was called.

The tone for aggression was set. And the foundation for bedlam had been laid.

Wallace and Artest then went at it, shoving and slapping each other. Players from both teams immediately came to the defense of their teammates, trying to separate the two—while also making it known there was no love lost for either side. As the initial scuffle seemed to be contained, referees separated the two sides and huddled, trying to determine who would be ejected and how to finish off the fewer than 90 seconds that remained in the game. While this was happening, Artest went and lay down on the scorer's table.

What happened next changed the way American sports events are conducted.

"I was lying down when I got hit with a liquid," Artest—who would later change his name to Metta World Peace—would tell ESPN sideline reporter Jim Gray in a phone interview that night. "Ice and glass on my chest and on my face. After that, it was self-defense."

The crowd at the Palace was stirring into a frenzy by this point. John Green, a fan in the lower bowl of the arena, threw a drink at Artest, which was a direct hit. Artest immediately flew into the stands in a rage, going after the fan he mistakenly believed threw it. Teammate Stephen Jackson followed him into the seats, punching another fan in the face. At this point, all hell broke loose with players, coaches, and team personnel from both sides entering the stands to retrieve (or retaliate against) players. Bottles, cups, food—anything at this point became a flying object— raining down on the court. Fans then tried to get in cheap shots, running onto the court to try to fight Artest, who was being escorted off.

It was a full-blown melee, on display for the entire nation to see right around the hour that most newscasts on the East Coast were about to begin their 11 p.m. broadcasts. The game was ended by the refereeing crew, with 45.9 seconds remaining.

"I said, 'Holy ----,'" former NBA commissioner David Stern said in the oral history. "And then I called (former deputy commissioner) Russ (Granik) and said, 'Are you watching our 'blank' game?' He said no. I said, 'Well, turn our 'blank' game on. You're not gonna believe it.'"

. . . the fallout from the brawl would be unprecedented in American sports . . .

After all was said and done, the NBA was left with a tremendous public black eye. The league— still fighting to figure out its reputation in the post–Michael Jordan era—was branded as a league full of thugs and criminals. The next day, the NBA would suspend Artest, O'Neal, Jackson, and Wallace indefinitely.

Eventually, the fallout from the brawl would be unprecedented in American sports: Nine players were suspended by the NBA, with Artest suspended for the remainder of the season and Jackson (30 games) and O'Neal (15 games) being hit hard as well. A total of 146 games were lost by players on both teams and nearly $11 million in fines levied. Artest alone was fined nearly $5 million, and O'Neal $4.1 million. Five Pacers players—O'Neal, Artest, Jackson, David Harrison, and Anthony Johnson—were charged with assault and battery, eventually pleading no contest.

The NBA—and other professional sports leagues—increased the layers of security between players and fans throughout its arenas, in addition to modifying alcohol sales practices.

"This was certainly one of the most difficult events that we encountered," Granik told *USA Today* in 2014. "We had never seen anything like this. We realized immediately that it's going to have a very large impact on the league and it would require a very significant response. I don't think there was any doubt about that."

MIAMI HEAT'S "BIG THREE"

Championships Become a Team-Up Sport

The nature of free agency in sports is that once you become one, you are *free* to pick where you want to play. When it started in baseball, then moved throughout the professional sports leagues in the United States, it changed the way players, teams, and leagues do business. But it had, for the most part, remained a solo endeavor. When your time came, you explored your options and made your choice.

You did. You hardly ever consulted anyone else.

And then the offseason of 2010 came along.

For years, franchises had been positioning themselves for this one. It was a Halley's Comet of sorts in the basketball transaction world. The reason? The draft class of 2003—considered one of the best in history—were approaching their time to test the market. In addition, a number of other established stars had the ability to opt out of their current deals and seek new ones. Teams began moving assets and pieces (and most importantly, money) around beginning as early as three years before, trying to be in the best spot to land a player who could transform a team.

A *player*—singular.

Not players.

The marquee name on every team's wish list that summer was LeBron James. At only 25, James was already on his way to the Hall of Fame in Springfield, Massachusetts. He

On July 9, 2010, a fan grabs a poster featuring newly signed Miami Heat basketball players LeBron James, left, Dwyane Wade, center, and Chris Bosh, right.

was a two-time Most Valuable Player, far and away the best player on the planet, with a solid decade ahead of him in the prime of his career—maybe more. Getting a player of that caliber so early in his career could drastically change the direction of a franchise, even a city. But James wasn't the only one teams had their eyes on. Dwyane Wade, Chris Bosh, Dirk Nowitzki, Amar'e Stoudemire, Paul Pierce, and Ray Allen were all highly coveted.

To land any one of them would make a general manager's offseason. To land two of them? *Three of them?* Pure fantasy. Never going to happen.

That was, until LeBron James took his talents to South Beach.

It was a move that shocked the sporting world. James, a native son of Ohio, playing for his hometown Cleveland Cavaliers, decided to bolt for the Miami Heat. It seemed improbable at the time, because the Heat already had Wade—who had committed to re-sign. Two super-stars? Joining forces? The NBA had always been a tag-team league—Russell and Cousy, Reed and Frazier, Chamberlain and West, Johnson and Worthy, Bird and McHale, Jordan and Pippen, Robinson and Duncan, O'Neal and Bryant—but in most cases, those moves were made by the front office. A trade here, a draft pick there, and pretty soon a dynasty was created.

Players deciding which team they would make great was a concept that just hadn't been done before.

With James and Wade on board, the Miami Heat seemed set for the foreseeable future. But then word began circulating that they could finagle money and free up enough to sign Bosh. Three superstars, under the age of 30, all signing and playing together? Improbable. And yet, Miami was able to make it happen, simply because the players wanted it to happen.

They had begun conversations while a part of the US Olympic basketball team during the 2008 games in Beijing, China. James, Wade, and Bosh—all playing together, all playing big

"We were just ourselves. All we did was pretty much talk. We told him how things would be, how we operated and how he would fit in. He would fit right in. He's a team guy. That's who he really is. We told him he wouldn't have to change anything and we wouldn't have to change anything for him. He just fits right in."—*Stephen Curry talking to the* San Jose Mercury News *after Kevin Durant joined the Warriors*

AND ONE!

roles in America's first gold medal after the embarrassing third-place finish in 2004—did the math and realized their contracts all expired the same summer. They had formed friendships not only by being the young faces of the NBA, but because of these transformative games. There were still two seasons to go, but the idea of playing together was certainly intriguing.

Most never believed it possible because with only 13 players on a roster, basketball is a sport of egos and three big ones in one locker room seemed to be a recipe for disaster—no matter how good of friends you are.

The trickle-down effect even reached the high school and college ranks.

Once the moves were made and the dust settled, the Heat had been the chosen team for three of the league's biggest stars. Critics and angry fans chided it as a cheap way to win a championship ring. But in the NBA, collecting superstars is the way to winning. Pretty soon, team-up acts began popping up all over the league.

Carmelo Anthony, fresh off a new deal in Denver, pushed to get traded to the New York Knicks to join Stoudemire. Chris Paul would later push for a trade to the Clippers to join budding young star Blake Griffin. Dwight Howard would go to Houston to team up with James Harden. Any solo star on a bad team immediately was pegged as the next potential tag-team partner for whatever lonely star played on a good team. The trickle-down effect even reached the high school and college ranks.

In 2014, heralded top recruit Jahlil Okafor said he would only play at whatever school his friend —fellow top prospect, Tyus Jones—was going to. They would be a package deal. Duke won the sweepstakes for both . . . and then won the national championship a few months later. Athletes like winning, and what better way to do that than by controlling where you and a friend end up?

For the Heat, it was a boon. Even though the trio orchestrated a gaudy, over-the-top roll-out celebration where they boasted of winning championship after championship after championship until they essentially would become bored with it, the plan worked. In the four years that the "Big Three" were together in Miami, the Heat went to the NBA Finals each year, winning twice —2011-12 and 2012-13—before James opted out and became a free agent in 2014.

Some say their plan was a bust, because three players of their caliber should have won the title every year they played together. Instead, it was only two titles in four years. James, considered the ringleader in the decision, decided that the foray into team-up championships had been fulfilled and returned to Cleveland.

But not before already having Kyrie Irving in place and then recruiting Kevin Love to join them.

REBRANDING AS THE "NBA FINALS"

A Name Change for the League's Ultimate Showcase

NO. **47**

The numbers were bleak. Each year, the NBA would roll out its playoffs with a cadre of stars, personalities and matchups that lived up to the hype. It was the end of the 1970s and the NBA had finally seemed to shed itself of the staid and boring image that it owned before the merger with the American Basketball Association in 1976. There were exciting players, which meant that once its postseason began, there would be a golden opportunity to show the American sports fan just how fun the NBA had become.

Each year, the American sports fan's response was the same: *What else is on?*

It's true. The title series to decide the NBA champion was not must-see-TV. In fact, it was hardly on live TV at all, as the league's network partner CBS decided to air many of the games on tape delay. Nobody was watching. Part of the problem? The NBA had no idea what to actually call the series that would decide its champion.

"It just didn't resonate," said Brian McIntyre, the league's longtime communications man.

Major League Baseball had the World Series. The National Football League had the Super Bowl. The National Hockey League had the Stanley Cup. Even college basketball, the little cousin of the pros, had the Final Four.

The NBA? It stayed stuck in its ways, trotting out the "NBA World Championship Series" for 32 years. The name was a mouthful. It didn't roll off the tongue easily. It was easily

The Larry O'Brien Championship Trophy, showcased at the 2008 NBA Playoffs Symposium.

messed up, being the "NBA World Championship" or "NBA World Series." The name wasn't the reason that the television ratings plummeted to an all-time 6.7 average Nielsen rating in 1981. But it certainly wasn't doing the league any favors.

Two bona fide stars—Magic Johnson of the Los Angeles Lakers and Larry Bird of the Boston Celtics—had entered the league a year earlier. They provided an instant boost of attention and popularity to a league that needed it.

Just like that, the NBA finally had a name for its championship series.

Magic and the Lakers won the NBA title in 1980, but the ratings hardly budged much from the year prior, drawing an 8.0 rating. Bird and the Celtics won the following year, with the 6.7 rating and CBS preempting live coverage of four of the six games to show reruns of *The Incredible Hulk*, *The Dukes of Hazzard*, and *Dallas*.

Seriously.

"A lot of the newspaper guys ended up just calling it 'the finals,'" McIntyre recalled. "We went to newspapers, we went to TV—the networks—trying to drum up interest. Trying to see what would click. We didn't have as many assets as we have now. The NBA wasn't that big back then. But nothing resonated. Nothing took off."

Starting in 1983, in the rematch between the Lakers and Philadelphia 76ers, the NBA tried to push the moniker: *Showdown '83*. The ratings had doubled from 1981—up to 12.3—but the tagline felt forced. Nevertheless, the NBA used it again for the first title showdown between Magic's Lakers and Bird's Celtics. *Showdown '84* did the same number as the year prior, but it didn't seem to be catching on.

Everywhere you turned, it was still being referred to as "the finals." Even CBS ignored the NBA's push for rebranding, using "NBA World Championship" through both years in all of its television graphics packages. The league gave up on forcing "Showdown" down America's throats and went back to the "NBA World Championship Series" for 1985. (CBS, clearly not caring about partnership synergy, continued to drop the "series" from the name.)

McIntyre, who had joined the league office in 1981, was part of the team that attempted to come up with something that would replace the clunky "NBA World Championship Series" in time for the 1986 season.

"Mike Madden, when he was at the *Boston Globe* interviewed me in '84 and said, 'Hey, how come you guys can't come up with a name?'" McIntyre remembered. "I told him, 'Hey man, we've tried.' We had meetings left and right. We were going to call it *The Supreme Court* at one point. All kinds of things were thrown out, but they were all hokey."

Ever the resourceful public relations man, McIntyre listened to what the press had been doing for years.

"I said, 'Hey, why don't we just call it 'The NBA Finals?'" he says now, laughing about the exercises in futility to find a name. "If people have been calling it that, and keep calling it that, why don't we just call it that?"

Just like that, the NBA finally had a name for its championship series.

In 1986, with a clean logo—"The" and "Finals" were done in black cursive, with a red "1986" and blue "NBA" sandwiched in the middle—and little fanfare, the new name was unveiled. The Celtics and Rockets, who had met five years earlier in the lowest-rated finals series, met once again. The Celtics won, but most importantly, the series drew a 14.1 average Nielsen rating—the highest number since the ABA merger. CBS (clearly getting the hint) used the name in its graphics, and for the first time since 1980, didn't air any games on tape delay.

The clear, simplistic logo—designed by a friend of deputy commissioner Russ Granik's as a favor—was used for 10 years, before the NBA went to a logo featuring the Larry O'Brien Trophy from 1996 to 2002. In 2003, the league went back to the future, taking just the script "The Finals," which it has used ever since.

It is now one of the most iconic championship series logos in sports and stands alone among its professional sports brethren. All it took was 35 years to figure out that everyone else had already come up with it for them.

"When I saw Mike Madden a couple of years later, he commented that he liked the new name," McIntyre chuckled. "I told him, 'We thought about calling it the Stanley Bowl Series,' but people might've gotten mad, so we went with this instead."

On Watching NBA Finals Games on Tape Delay

"My dad had to wake me up at like 1:30 in the morning so I could see us celebrate three hours after we celebrated."
—*Bill Simmons,* Grantland

AND ONE!

ALLEN IVERSON

"The Answer"—A Man Full of Questions

"Michael! Get up on him!"

The call came from the bench of the Chicago Bulls. You can hear it if you find the tape on the Internet somewhere and listen closely enough. Phil Jackson, the Bulls head coach, saw a chance for his best defender to lock up a precocious rookie. In simple basketball terms, it was a good defensive player on a burgeoning offensive player. Only this wasn't simple basketball. This was Michael Jordan on Allen Iverson. One-on-one. At the top of the key.

March 12, 1997. If you weren't paying attention, it was just Game No. 63 for the Bulls and Game No. 62 for the 76ers. But in Philadelphia that night, it was a play—no, a move—that signaled the arrival of one of the great talents to enter the NBA.

It was the night that Iverson pulled the double-crossover on Jordan.

"A lot of guys, when you see guys that you kinda looked up to, they kinda shy away from the challenge," Iverson told the *Philadelphia Daily News* in 2013. "And I just took it on."

It was a glimpse of things to come for Iverson. He was the much-heralded No. 1 selection by the Sixers the previous summer, having wowed in his single season at Georgetown. Yes, Iverson had some baggage as he entered the pros, but he was an undeniable talent who had the game and swagger to back it up. No one really remembers much else from that game—Philadelphia lost 108–104, falling to 16-46, while the Bulls moved to 55-8, en route to championship No. 5. But maybe that's the perfect point to start trying to unwrap the riddle that was Allen Iverson.

A player defined by little snippets and clips and soundbites, without anyone remembering the context or the rest of the picture. There was the crossover of Jordan. The "Practice" rant. The stepping over an opposing player in the NBA Finals.

Allen Iverson in action on December 9, 2008.

But more than his moments of glory—or ignominy—Iverson broke the mold of what an NBA star should do and act like. He brought the streets to NBA arenas and into the living rooms of millions of basketball fans. After his first season with the Sixers, he no longer began to resemble the clean-cut, mostly ink-free black basketball star that no one thought twice about. Iverson would soon wear his hair in cornrow braids, cover his body in tattoos, dress like he went home every night to his hometown of Hampton, Virginia.

There will always be the question of "What if?" surrounding Iverson.

And yet, he became more and more popular. From the moment it opened in 1998 through its first decade, the NBA Store in Manhattan kept track of the most popular player jersey flying off store shelves. Number one on the list was Michael Jordan. Number two was Kobe Bryant.

Allen Iverson was No. 3.

He started the trend of wearing a sleeve on one arm while playing. His sneaker line with Reebok lasted for 13 years. In 2013, LeBron James said of Iverson: "Pound for pound, probably the greatest player ever to play the game." The legend of Iverson is one of admiration and confusion.

"There might not be a more polarizing player to pull for in NBA history," said *Washington Post* sportswriter Kent Babb, author of *Not A Game: The Incredible Rise and Unthinkable Fall of Allen Iverson*. "He is simultaneously one of the best athletes to ever pick up a basketball and one of the most complicated men to follow off the court. One is poetry, the other is a car crash."

How could a player so talented and so beloved, simply disappear from the league? Iverson only played in 14 NBA seasons—the latter two as a disgruntled bit player with the Denver Nuggets, Detroit Pistons, and Memphis Grizzlies before finally retiring with the 76ers in 2010. He ranks 23rd on the NBA's all-time scoring list with 24,368 points. He won the Most Valuable Player Award in 2001.

And yet, his fall from grace has been as mesmerizing as his rise to popularity.

He reportedly practiced with hangovers while in Philadelphia. And when he wasn't hung over, he was out getting drunk at bars and clubs all over the city. He would skip team functions, publicly berate coaches, refuse to adhere to the NBA's dress code. Basically, he became a person who thumbed his nose at anyone who tried to make him conform.

"This is why I feel like it's just another obstacle in my life," Iverson told *Slam* magazine in 2010, when asked if he grew tired of more being expected of him. "I mean, it's just something else to try and overcome. If people don't understand me, if people have a negative feeling about me and they don't even know me, so be it. But I mean, I'm not that way—I wish people wouldn't think of me as some type of bad person, 'cause I'm not. But I mean, if they choose to feel that way about me 'cause of what they read and what they hear, there's nothing I can do about that."

Iverson may have worn out his welcome in the NBA, but he certainly lived up to the hype that preceded him as a rookie.

At 6'0", he did things against bigger, stronger, more gifted players that no one had seen before. He single-handedly dragged the 76ers to the 2001 NBA Finals against a superior Los Angeles Lakers team. In that finals, Iverson was his team's leading scorer every night, totaling 178 points—still an NBA record for a five-game series.

There will always be the question of "What if?" surrounding Iverson. What if he hadn't let his personal demons get the best of him? What if he hadn't burned virtually every bridge in the league? What if he didn't become so wrapped up in living up to the persona that he created and fit in like every other star in the NBA's universe? All of those valid and worthy questions to ask about the career of the man who provided so many highlights to counter-balance.

The one answer—perhaps the definitive answer—is that had he done all of those things, Allen Iverson never would have been Allen Iverson.

On Missing a Sixers Practice in 2002

"We're sitting here, and I'm supposed to be the franchise player, and we're talking about practice. I mean listen, we're sitting here talking about practice. Not a game. Not a game. But we're talking about practice. Not the game that I go out there and die for and play every game like it's my last, but we're talking about practice man. How silly is that?"—*Allen Iverson*

AND ONE!

NBA JAM
A One Billion Dollar Success

"Would any of you guys like to be in a video game?"

Stephen Howard still remembers the absurdity of the question. He was working out at old Alumni Hall on DePaul's campus in the spring of 1992, trying to stay in shape for a shot at the NBA. Howard had just finished his collegiate career, but was considered a fringe player at best. So, when a guy with jeans and long, curly hair walked into the gym with the proposition of being a part of a video game, Howard and some friends thought it must have been a gag.

NO. **49**

He loved playing video games in college, so Howard immediately jumped on the offer, pulling a friend who had been a walk-on for the Blue Demons along with him. The mystery man gave them the details: They would be paid $12 an hour for their time (though since Howard had a chance at the pros, he got $24), and would begin filming in a couple of weeks at a warehouse on the South Side of Chicago.

Howard asked for the man's name.

"Mark Turmell," he said. "I'm creating an arcade basketball game."

Howard then asked what it was going to be called.

"*NBA Jam.*"

It has been almost 25 years since the arcade game that changed sports video games was released to the public. Turmell's brainchild, developed through Midway Games, turned arcade games upside-down. Its unique brand of high-flying, colorful, out-of-this-world play immediately captured the attention of kids—and adults—all over the world when it debuted in the summer of 1993. The game still holds the world record for most money earned, as one machine pulled in $2,468 (or 9,782 quarters) in a single day.

In its first year alone, the game earned over a billion dollars in quarters.

The success of the *NBA Jam* arcade game was unprecedented, as it broke all kinds of records, including earning over a billion dollars in quarters.

"It does sound a bit crazy," Turmell said, "but after that game came out, we had so many people write us or tell us that, 'I wasn't a fan of the NBA before, but after playing the game for a while I'm now a big fan of the NBA.' So I think it actually did usher in a new set of fans to the sport and various athletes."

It's true. *NBA Jam*'s game-play and entertainment factor were unlike anything developed and plopped in an arcade before. Two-man teams consisting of real NBA players—the first time that the NBA had allowed its license to be used for an arcade game—made the feel of the game radically different than any of its predecessors. It wasn't just that the two-on-two play made for the perfect arcade component; it was the over-the-top action that earned it legions of followers.

From the super-high dunking abilities, to the ability of a player to get red-hot from 3-point range—*NBA Jam* broke every rule in the book.

"There was a different energy about it," said Tim Kitzrow, who provided the voice effects for the game. "We talked about it being larger than life. That this was the superhero, comic-book version of the NBA. And that's what differentiates it."

In fact, it was Kitzrow's catch phrases—He's heating up! Razzle dazzle! He's on fire! and the famous, BOOMSHAKALAKA!—that made the game feel out of this world. Kitzrow had been doing voice-overs for pinball and arcade games before he hooked up with Turmell. But once he saw the vision that Turmell had for *NBA Jam*, he knew that it was going to be an instant hit.

The NBA initially had some trepidation about allowing Midway Games to use the license, because the league felt there was an unsavory element in video arcades. They had a perception

On What Happened When Michael Jordan Found Out about *NBA Jam*'s Popularity

"Jordan was ticked that he wasn't in the game, so his people made a call to Mark. I came in to do the voice of Jordan, and Midway made and shipped off a separate console just for him. So somewhere in the universe, exists the one *NBA Jam* arcade game that has Michael Jordan in it."—*Tim Kitzrow*

AND ONE!

of arcade parlors in cities being littered with gangs and teenage criminals, so at first the NBA balked at allowing the game to continue. But once Turmell made a crudely produced video showing arcades that catered to families, the league relented, allowing Midway to continue. From there, it was all about trying to make the game as unique as possible.

Midway was on the cutting-edge of the video game industry with digitized video motion techniques, which allowed them to capture life-like movements of their models. Which was why the services of Howard—who would later play for the Utah Jazz—and the handful of other college basketball players used, were so important. They provided the template for the movements of Patrick Ewing or John Stockton or Scottie Pippen.

The real-life quality, combined with the cartoonish effects, made for the perfect storm.

"You could tell it was going to be cool," Howard remembered. "Like we would do all types of things. We would have to sit on the end of the bench, hold a ball and then tumble on to this mat—and that's what ended up being the flips when you would dunk in the game. They had this little 7-foot goal that we would use for dunks, so you could be really elaborate with it. All the stuff that's in the game is just us in the warehouse."

The real-life quality, combined with the cartoonish effects, made for the perfect storm. NBA players couldn't get enough of it, with arcade consoles being shipped to locker rooms all over the league. (Shaquille O'Neal, then a rookie for the Orlando Magic, bought two—one which he kept at home, and the other for using when the team was on the road. It was packed up and shipped to every destination so he and teammates could play.) Today, consoles can sell for thousands of dollars if they're in good, working condition. Even as the game spawned sequels and different variations for home consoles like Sega Genesis and Super Nintendo, the original arcade version is still considered the best.

"The following year after Jam came out, I was back at Midway to do voice-overs for another video game," Kitzrow said. "There's an article on a bulletin board that says, '*NBA Jam* tops one billion dollars in sales' and I'm absolutely convinced someone had typed that up as a joke. It was so ridiculous. And I said, 'Who wrote this?' They said, 'No, seriously. It's true. It made a billion in quarters.' To this day, I still cannot believe that."

THE BREAKS OF THE GAME

A Legendary Journalist Makes the Sport Come to Life

It begins with the most minute of details: the motel. The roster of the Portland Trail Blazers, all checking in to the sleepy community of Gresham, Oregon, in preparation for training camp for the 1979-80 season. Two years earlier, the Trail Blazers had been on top of the world, winning the NBA championship behind the play of superstar center Bill Walton and the guile of head coach Jack Ramsay. But by the time writer David Halberstam showed up, much had changed. The team had effectively started from scratch.

So Halberstam began with the motel.

The result, more than a year later, would become *The Breaks of the Game*—one of the seminal works in sports literature, certainly in the basketball category. Halberstam, a master of prose of the highest order, chronicles the journey of Portland's season. More than that, Halberstam brought his reporter's lens to the world of sports books, ushering in a new era of embedded reporting for nonfiction work that still percolates to this day.

Writers and reporters had sidled themselves alongside teams and players and coaches before, but rarely to the degree that Halberstam did. Already a Pulitzer Prize–winning reporter through his work for the *New York Times* in Vietnam during the war, Halberstam had been writing books for almost two decades by the time he ventured to Oregon to tag along with the Trail Blazers. His first real hit, however, wouldn't come until 1972's *The Best*

Author David Halberstam works at his office in New York City on May 14, 1993.

and the Brightest, and from there, Halberstam hit his stride and won critical acclaim. But he had not dabbled in the world of sports.

Riding shotgun to the chaotic, often-dysfunctional season the Blazers endured changed all that. And changed the way writers covered and wrote about the NBA.

. . . it was enough for Halberstam to dip his toes in the sportswriting waters and stay there.

Bill Simmons, who has chronicled the league as much as anyone in the last 20 years, has often cited *The Breaks of the Game* as the reason he first dipped his toe in the sportswriting waters. He was a die-hard Celtics fan in Massachusetts growing up, when he was introduced to Halberstam's masterpiece. Once he started, he couldn't stop. It's a tale often repeated by those who read the book during their formative years.

"I didn't understand how to write," Simmons wrote in a 2007 column espousing his adoration for the book. "I had written short stories as a little kid, read every book in sight, even finished every Hardy Boys book before I turned 10. But I didn't know how to write. *Breaks of the Game* was the first big-boy book I ever loved. Within a few pages, I came to believe that he wrote the book just for me. I plowed through it in one weekend. A few months later, I read it again. Eventually, I read the book so many times that the spine of the book crumbled, so I bought the paperback version to replace it."

Simmons' column on the book would eventually be reprinted as the introduction to the re-released paperback version in 2009. It's not hard to see why he and others fell for it. Halberstam delivers every nuance about the Trail Blazers to the reader in dripping detail. Rarely are individuals quoted—rather Halberstam connects the dots using observations and reported details.

The finished product is a guide to detail-rich reporting that countless writers have used as a model for how to tell stories in and around the league since its release in 1981. In the *New York Times* review shortly after its release, Christopher Lehmann-Haupt called the book "one of the best books I've ever read about American sports." In 2002, *Sports Illustrated* cited it as one of the top 100 sports books ever written—checking in at No. 17. Sure, there are other basketball books that were ranked higher on that list—notably, *A Season on the Brink* by John Feinstein—but Halberstam's helped pave the way for books like Feinstein's to be possible. To gain the access (and trust) required to be around a team for an entire season, while not having any restrictions as to what you can print, is tantamount to gold for a journalist.

Halberstam, who died suddenly in a car accident in 2007, never divulged exactly why he chose the Trail Blazers or the NBA to be his first foray into the sports world. Maybe it was the absence of Walton (who had been traded after the 1978 season to the Clippers). Maybe it was the presence of Ramsay—a former college coach who had found immediate success upon transferring to the pros, but was looking to capture that championship streak. Maybe it was the cast of characters—from transient players like Steve Hayes and Greg Bunch to the veterans like Maurice Lucas and Kermit Washington—that made Portland an attractive target. Or quite simply, it could have just been that the Trail Blazers gave Halberstam the access that others didn't.

Whatever the case, it was enough for Halberstam to dip his toes in the sportswriting waters and stay there. Next came books about Olympic rowing (*The Amateurs*), baseball (*Summer of '49*, *October 1964*, *The Teammates*), and football (*The Education of a Coach*, *The Glory Game*). Before his death, Halberstam revisited the NBA once more—the subject this time was Michael Jordan in *Playing For Keeps: Michael Jordan and the World He Made*—once again showing the delicate and deft touch required when reporting on one of the world's most popular sports. (For what it's worth, Halberstam's book on Jordan—done with his agreement, but without any sit-down interviews with him—is considered one of the best books on Jordan ever written.)

Still, it all started with *The Breaks of the Game* and showcasing the true life behind the league that few knew existed: a snapshot of a growing league, during a transitional time in American culture, captured by one of the masterful storytellers of the last 50 years.

Read all 362 pages of it and you're bound to find out why.

"He was 73 years-old, a Pulitzer winner, the first respected journalist to question the war in Vietnam. I'm not sure what made him decide to tackle the NBA, but there hasn't been a better basketball book before or since. He nailed everything. He picked the perfect season for the perfect league—Magic and Bird's rookie year—and took a 362-page snapshot of a professional sport right as it was shifting from a downtrodden era to a lucrative one. Maybe the timing was incredible, but so was the work itself. And it changed my life for the better."— *Bill Simmons, ESPN.com*

AND ONE!

ACKNOWLEDGMENTS

Writing a book is hard work. Writing a book trying to encapsulate the entire history of the sport of basketball is incredibly hard. This is not a cry for pity, just letting you know that the book you've just digested was the product of nearly a year of intense writing sessions, interviews, and most of all—time.

A hearty thanks to Keith Wallman and the wonderful folks at Lyons Press for not only choosing me to take on this project, but for providing a steady guiding hand throughout it all. I would also be remiss in not thanking the truly superb Cranford Public Library, in my hometown of Cranford, New Jersey. It's a place where I grew up loving and devouring books, and where I spent so many days in quiet writing my own.

When I took on this book project, I was a sportswriter looking for work. I had spent nearly nine years at the *Newark Star-Ledger*—my home newspaper—covering everything under the sun. The confidence in my writing and storytelling skills is due mainly to two people, who took me under their watchful eyes and showed a young kid out of college how it's done: Steve Politi and Tom Luicci. Thanks also to James Montgomery of *Rolling Stone*, Melissa Hoppert of the *New York Times* and B. J. Schecter of *Sports Illustrated*—their encouragement while I worked as a freelancer helped make the writing in this book feel full of life. An additional round of thanks to my new bosses Chris Brienza and David Cooper at Coyne PR, who helped me connect with folks from their NBA days.

My family—from my mother (whom I got the journalism bug from) and father (love of sports)—this book is a product of you both. My brothers, in-laws, friends, all of you kept me going throughout this process.

Finally, Team Prunty on my homefront. My wife, whose relentless support of this book— from giving me time to work on it to being my first line of defense in reading it through—you are my rock in every sense of the word. And to my wonderful daughter Quinn: This book is for you. There will come a day when I hope you read it all, and know that you were the inspiration to write it. Seeing your joy and love for books inspired me to write one you can read in the future and know that your dad's name is on the front. I can see already that you have the inquisitive and sport-loving genes from your old man. Hopefully you have your mother's athletic ones, though. That's why when I was picking out which sport to try out first, before you even turned a year old, it was an easy decision.

You got a basketball.

SOURCES AND INTERVIEWS

Sources

5.

Curti, Chuck. "ABA Feature—ABA Shed Inferior Image to Help Change NBA." *Beaver County Times*, June 14, 2001.

Goldpaper, Sam. "Pro Basketball Leagues Merge; New York Retains Two Teams." *New York Times*, June 18, 1976.

Murphy, Michael. "The ABA Way: For Pure Entertainment, American Basketball Association Was a Slam Dunk." *Houston Chronicle*, 1996.

4.

Cobbs, Chris, and *Los Angeles Times*. "Widespread Cocaine Use by Players Alarms NBA." *Washington Post*, August 20, 1980.

Johnson, Roy S. "Two Great Rivalries Resume: Bird-Johnson, Celtics-Lakers." *New York Times*, May 28, 1984.

Medina, Mark. "Magic Johnson on Larry Bird: 'We're Mirrors of Each Other.'" *Los Angeles Times*, April 12, 2012.

Warner, Rick. "Bird vs. Magic: Their 1979 Matchup Took TV Ratings to Still Unequaled High." Associated Press, April 2, 1989.

3.

Associated Press. "Wooden Dies at Age 99." ESPN.com, June 7, 2010.

"Reaction to John Wooden's Death." NBA News on NBA.com, June 5, 2010.

2.

"50th Birthday Jordan." NBA.com, Chicago Bulls, February 14, 2013.

Associated Press. "Jordan Purchase of Bobcats Approved." ESPN.com, March 17, 2010.

Brown, Tim. "Michael Jordan's .202 Batting Average Source of Pride for His Ex-Manager Terry Francona." Yahoo! Sports, February 13, 2013.

Fatsis, Stefan. "NBA Bravely Plans for the Day When Michael Jordan Retires." *Wall Street Journal*, February 6, 1998.

Willigan, Geraldine E. "High-Performance Marketing: An Interview with Nike's Phil Knight." *Harvard Business Review*, Jul-Aug 1992.

1.

Amick, Sam. "Team USA's Barcelona Return Shows Basketball's Shift of Power Since Dream Team." *USA Today*, September 8, 2014.

Whitaker, Lang. "The Dream Will Never Die: An Oral History of the Dream Team." *GQ*, June 11, 2012.

6.

Aldridge, David. "Oral History: The Life and Times of Commissioner David Stern." NBA.com, January 27, 2014.

Lombardo, John. "The Making of a Legacy: David Stern Used Tenacity and Vision to Redefine the Role of Commissioner." *Street & Smith's SportsBusiness Journal*, January 20, 2014.

7.

Montville, Leigh. "In the Nick of Time." *Sports Illustrated*, November 6, 1989.

Sachare, Alex. "The Rules: 24-Second Clock Revived the Game." NBA.com, NBA Encyclopedia Playoff Edition.

8.

Haberstroh, Tom. "How the NBA Learned to Stop Worrying and Love the Bomb." ESPN.com, June 3, 2015.

Ryan, Bob. "Unfortunately, the 3-Pointer Is Here to Stay." *Boston Globe*, January 30, 2016.

9.

Dosh, Kristi. "Is EA Sports Revenue Worth Schools' Risk?" ESPN.com, August 21, 2013.

"Ed O'Bannon Press Conference Quotes." BD Global, August 9, 2014.

Wetzel, Dan. "Making NCAA Pay?" Yahoo! Sports, July 21, 2009.

10.

Broussard, Chris. "Pro Basketball: A Game Played Above the Rim, Above All Else." *New York Times*, February 15, 2004.

Caponi-Tabery, Gena. *Jump for Joy: Jazz, Basketball & Black Culture in 1930s America*. Amherst: University of Massachusetts Press, 2008.

11.

Abramson, Mitch. "Jason Collins Hopes Other Gay Athletes Follow His Lead and Come Out While Still Playing." *New York Daily News*, February 12, 2015.

Barry, Dan. "A Sports Executive Leaves the Safety of His Shadow Life." *New York Times*, May 15, 2011.

Collins, Jason. "Why NBA Center Jason Collins Is Coming Out Now." *Sports Illustrated*, May 6, 2013.

12.

Bova, Dan. "Magic Johnson Names His Dream Pick-Up Team." *Maxim*, November 21, 2013.

MacMullan, Jackie. "Magic Crisis Showed Stern's Strength." ESPN.com, January 31, 2014.

Moughty, Sarah. "20 Years After HIV Announcement, Magic Johnson Emphasizes: 'I Am Not Cured.'" *Frontline*, PBS.com, November 7, 2011.

Springer, Steve. "Painful Moment, Remarkable Journey." ESPN.com, November 7, 2011.

13.

Cantu, Rick. "After 50 Years, Miners' Historic Victory Still Resonates in Basketball." *Austin American-Statesman*, April 2, 2016.

Forgrave, Red. "50 Years Ago, Texas Western Didn't Realize What It Set in Motion." FoxSports.com, February 5, 2016.

Norwood, Robyn. "Don Haskins, 78: Basketball Coach Was First to Win NCAA Title With 5 Black Starters." *Los Angeles Times*, September 8, 2008.

14.

Harlem Globetrotters: The Team That Changed the World documentary.

15.

Papanek, John. "A Different Drummer: Getting Inside the Mind of Kareem Abdul-Jabbar." *Sports Illustrated*, March 31, 1980.

17.

Rogin, Gilbert. "They All Boo When Celtics Legend Red Auerbach Sits Down." *Sports Illustrated*, April 5, 1965.

18.

Blinebury, Fran. "50 Years Later, Wilt's Mark on the NBA is Unmistakable." NBA.com, NBA History, May 21, 2012.

"NBA's Greatest Moments: Wilt Scores 100!" NBA.com, NBA Encyclopedia Playoff Edition.

Pomerantz, Gary M. *Wilt, 1962: The Night of 100 Points and the Dawn of a New Era*. Three Rivers Press, 2005.

19.

Keim, John, Mike Rodak, et al. "Is LeBron James the Best Athlete in the World?" ESPN.com, June 15, 2015.

20.

"Ohio State's Oley Olsen: Forefather of Final Four." *Legends Quarterly*, March 30, 2014.

21.

Crowe, Jerry. "That Iconic NBA Silhouette Can Be Traced Back to Him." *Los Angeles Times*, April 27, 2010.

22.

Katz, Andy, and Associated Press. "Hall of Famer Dave Gavitt Dies at 73." ESPN.com, September 17, 2011.

25.

Peter, Josh. "Error Jordan: Key Figures Still Argue Over Who Was Responsible for Nike Deal." *USA Today*, September 30, 2015.

26.

Associated Press. "Pro Bosses Okay Laker L.A. Move." *Sarasota Journal*, February 26, 1960.

Howard, Johnette. "Why Minneapolis Lakers' Loss to Globetrotters Was So Meaningful." ESPN.com, August 25, 2016.

"Jerry West Q&A: Reflecting on 20 Years of Kobe Bryant." ESPN.com, January 15, 2015.

27.

Goldaper, Sam. "All Eyes On Lottery For Ewing." *New York Times*, May 6, 1985.

McManis, Sam. "NBA's New Showtime: It's Called The Lottery." *Los Angeles Times*, May 14, 1985.

28.

Associated Press. "Bill Russell Says Hate Is Rule in Boston." *Gettysburg Times*, June 23, 1966.

Deford, Frank. "The Ring Leader: Bill Russell Helped the Celtics Rule Their Sport Like No Team Ever Has." *Sports Illustrated*, May 10, 1999.

NBA.com live chat with Bill Russell, 2005, www.nba.com/celtics/chat/russell_050228.html.

"Wilt Chamberlain and Bill Russell Interview by Ahmad Rashad, 1997." https://www.youtube.com/watch?v=kdd2biHVlyA.

29.

Lincicome, Bernie. "Dislike Michigan? Count the Ways." *Chicago Tribune*, April 5, 1993.

Van Stratt, Gillian. "Jalen Rose Says Michigan Has Failed at Honoring Those Who Helped Build Program, Specifically the Fab Five." MLive.com, January 24, 2014.

Wieberg, Steve. "Fab Five Anniversary Falls Short of Fondness." *USA Today*, March 28, 2002.

30.

Markazi, Arash. "Showtime Lakers Weren't Built Overnight." ESPN.com, February 18, 2011.

Olstler, Scott, and Steve Springer. "Fast Company: When It's Showtime at the Forum, the Lakers May Be the Stars But Jerry Buss Is the Director." *Los Angeles Times*, November 30, 1986.

Schrager, Peter. "The Drugs, Sex, and Swagger of the 1980s Lakers—Plus How They'd Match Up to the Miami Heat Today." *GQ*, March 18, 2014.

31.

Goldpaper, Sam. "NBA Will Ban Drug Users." *New York Times*, September 29, 1983.

———. "O'Brien Steps Down as Commissioner of NBA." *New York Times*, November 10, 1983.

Lambert, Pam. "Larry O'Brien: 'What Makes a Winning Team.'" *Ocala* (FL) *Star-Banner*, May 21, 1978.

32.

Dutch, Taylor. "How Duke vs. UNC Became the Best Rivalry in College Basketball." *Bleacher Report*, March 7, 2014.

Watson, Graham. "US Rep. Brad Miller: 'If Duke Was Playing the Taliban, I'd Have to Pull for the Taliban.'" Yahoo! Sports, March 24, 2012.

33.

Jenks, Jayson. "The Rules of the Game." Grantland.com, March 22, 2012.

34.

Coffey, Wayne. "Global Warning: NBA's Foreign Invasion Exposes Problems in Homeland Hoops." *New York Daily News*, July 14, 2002.

Lee, Michael. "The NBA's European Invasion." *Washington Post*, April 1, 2007.

35.

Lieberman, Nancy. "One of the Guys." *The Players' Tribune*, October 28, 2015.

Narducci, Mark. "Lieberman Is Enjoying Her Summer in the USBL." *Philadelphia Inquirer*, July 21, 1986.

36.

Garry, Peter. "The Net-Ripping, Backboard-Shaking, Mind-Blowing Dr. J." *Sports Illustrated*, December 11, 1972.

37.

Freeman, Scott. "The Shoes Make the Man." *Indianapolis Monthly*, April 2006.

Marchese, David. "Chucks & Bucks: An Oral History of the Coolest Shoes on Earth." *Spin*, September 10, 2012.

38.

"Jerry West Q&A: Reflecting on 20 Years of Kobe Bryant." ESPN.com, January 15, 2015.

39.

Sims, David. "*Boys Among Men* and the NBA's High-School Boom." *The Atlantic*, March 22, 2016.

41.

Deveny, Sean. "Q&A with the Star of 'The White Shadow.'" *Sporting News*, November 21, 2005.

Handel, Jonathan. "'White Shadow' Ken Howard Remembered Courtside in Turkey." *Hollywood Reporter*, April 1, 2016.

Simmons, Bill. "Genius in the 'Shadow.'" ESPN.com, Page 2, October 4, 2002.

42.

Clayton, Mark. "Canadians Gear Up For NBA Expansion Team." *Christian Science Monitor*, September 29, 1993.

Crossman, Matt. "'The Place Went Nuts': An Oral History of the 1988 Charlotte Hornets." *Charlotte Magazine*, October 17, 2013.

43.

Dews, Fred. "Yao Ming at Brookings—Basketball Links So Many People in the U.S. and China." *Brookings Now*, March 28, 2014.

Fussman, Cal. "Next Athlete: Yao Ming." *ESPN the Magazine*, December 25, 2000.

McCallum, Jack. "Yao Ming's Cultural Impact Made Him a Certain Hall of Fame Inductee," 2016. SI.com.

Thamel, Pete. "The NBA and China Are Fans of Each Other." *New York Times*, August 9, 2008.

44.

Eisenberg, Jeff. "Impatient Duke Fans Once Wanted Mike Krzyzewski Fired." Yahoo! Sports, January 23, 2015.

O'Neil, Dana. "Duke, Coach K Figured Out How to Rule a New World." ESPN.com, April 7, 2015.

45.

Abrams, Jonathan. "The Malice at the Palace." Grantland.com, March 20, 2012.

Buckner, Candace. "As 'Malice at the Palace' Brawl Turns 10, Impact Lasts." *USA Today*, November 18, 2014.

47.

Simmons, Bill. "NBA Mailbag: This Is the End." Grantland.com, April 11, 2014.

48.

Perner, Mark. "The Night Allen Iverson Crossed Up Michael Jordan." *Philadelphia Daily News*, March 1, 2013.

Slam Staff. "The Infamous." *Slam* Online, January 9, 2010.

50.

Simmons, Bill. "A Tribute to the Ultimate Teacher." ESPN.com, Page 2, April 28, 2014.

Interviews

Val Ackerman, Kent Babb, Len Elmore, Billy Goodwin, Mark Heisler, Stephen Howard, Tim Kitzrow, Rebecca Lobo, Tom McElroy, Brian McIntyre, Sean McManus, Reggie Miller, Jim Nantz, Ben Osborne, John Paquette, Jim Riswold, Howard Smith, Jim Spanarkel, Carol Stiff, C. Vivian Stringer, Mark Turmell, Peter Vecsey, Grant Wahl, Pat Williams

INDEX

PHOTO CREDITS

Panel page: AP Photo
Opposite Copyright: GYRO PHOTOGRAPHY/amanaimagesRF
Introduction: Library of Congress
End of Introduction: Official White House Photo by Pete Souza
--

5. The ABA: AP Photo/Richard Drew
4. Bird-Magic Rivalry: AP Photo/Mark J. Terrill; background ThinkStock
3. John Wooden: Photo courtesy of CoachWooden.com
2. Michael Jordan: AP Photo/John Swart; background ThinkStock
1. The Dream Team: AP Photo/John Gaps III; background ThinkStock
--

6. David Stern: Photograph by Kevin Maloney/Fortune Brainstorm Tech, CC BY 2.0, https://commons.wikimedia.org/w/index.php?curid=20398544
7. 24-Second Shot Clock: U.S. Army photo by Anthony Langley / Flickr Commons / https://flic.kr/p/huW3QG
8. 3-Point Shot: AP Photo/L.M. Otero; background ThinkStock
9. O'Bannon v. NCAA: AP Photo/Isaac Brekken
10. The Slam Dunk: AP Photo/Eric Risberg; background ThinkStock
11. Gay Players: AP Photo/Mark J. Terrill; background ThinkStock
12. Magic Johnson Diagnosed with HIV: AP Photo/Nick Ut; background ThinkStock
13. 1965-66 Texas Western Team: UTEP Athletics; background ThinkStock
14. Harlem Globetrotters: Library of Congress / Photo by Fred Palumbo; background ThinkStock
15. Kareem Abdul-Jabbar: AP Photo; background ThinkStock
16. NCAA Tournament Expands to 64 Teams: AP Photo/John Gaps III; background ThinkStock
17. Red Auerbach: Courtesy of Steve Lipofsky; background ThinkStock
18. Wilt Chamberlain: AP Photo/Paul Vathis, File; background ThinkStock
19. LeBron James: Flickr Commons Photo by Keith Allison/https://flic.kr/p/6cjPCB; background ThinkStock
20. Creation of the NCAA Tournament: Courtesy of the University of Oregon; background ThinkStock
21. The NBA Logo: AP Photo/Mary Altaffer
22. The Big East Conference: AP Photo/Henny Ray Abrams, File; background ThinkStock
23. The Final Four: AP Photo/David J. Phillip; background ThinkStock
24. Pat Summitt: Flickr Commons Photo by Aaron Vazquez, https://flic.kr/p/5JHKb5
25. Air Jordans: Courtesy of Nike; background ThinkStock
26. Lakers Move to Los Angeles: Wikimedia Commons / By Unknown - 1950-51 Minneapolis Lakers program, Public Domain, https://commons.wikimedia.org/w/index.php?curid=36123827
27. 1985 NBA Draft Lottery: AP Photo/Marty Lederhandler, File; background ThinkStock
28. Bill Russell: AP Photo/J.D. Lamontagne; background ThinkStock
29. The Fab Five: AP Photo/file; background ThinkStock

30. Showtime-era Lakers: AP Photo/Mark Terrill; background ThinkStock
31. Larry O'Brien: AP Photo/Dave Pickoff; background ThinkStock
32. Duke-North Carolina Rivalry: Courtesy of Duke University and the University of North Carolina
33. Phog Allen: AP Photo/Tom Sande
34. European Invasion: Flickr Commons Photo by Keith Allison / https://www.flickr.com/photos/keithallison/3996815319; background ThinkStock
35. Nancy Lieberman Plays in the USBL: AP Photo/Michael O'Brien; background ThinkStock
36. Julius Erving: AP Photo; background ThinkStock
37. Chuck Taylors: Flickr Commons Photo by Robert Valdemar / https://www.flickr.com/photos/tizen/4212531360; background ThinkStock
38. Kobe Bryant Trade: AP Photo/Susan Sterner, STf; background ThinkStock
39. High Schoolers in the NBA: AP Photo/Jim Mone; background ThinkStock
40. WNBA: Flickr Commons Photo by Keith Allison, https://www.flickr.com/photos/keithallison/5822935757/in/photostream/ and Flickr Commons Photo by Keith Allison, https://www.flickr.com/photos/keithallison/5822883059/in/photostream; background ThinkStock
41. The White Shadow: CBS Photo Archive/Getty Images; background ThinkStock
42. NBA Expansion: AP Photo/Marty Lederhandler; background ThinkStock
43. NBA Goes to Asia: Courtesy of Steve Lipofsky
44. Mike Krzyzewski: By D. Myles Cullen - This Image was released by the United States Department of Defense with the ID 120112-D-VO565-016 http://www.defense.gov/photoessays/photoessayss.aspx?id=2610, Public Domain, https://commons.wikimedia.org/w/index.php?curid=21502795
45. "Malice at the Palace": AP Photo/Oakland County Prosecutor; background ThinkStock
46. Miami Heat's "Big Three": AP Photo/Lynne Sladky
47. Rebranding as the "NBA Finals": By Rico Shen - Rico Shen, GFDL, https://commons.wikimedia.org/w/index.php?curid=4116107; background ThinkStock
48. Allen Iverson: Flickr Commons Photo by Keith Allison, https://flic.kr/p/5HHZ5m; background ThinkStock
49. NBA Jam: Photo by Foxparabola—Own Work, CC BY-SA 3.0, https://commons.wikimedia.org/w/index.php?corid=20045025
50. *The Breaks of the Game:* AP Photo/Mark Lennihan

ABOUT THE AUTHOR

Brendan Prunty has been a sportswriter since 2006, covering major sporting events and national figures. His work has appeared in the *New York Times*, *Sports Illustrated*, *Rolling Stone*, and the *Newark Star-Ledger* among other outlets. He has twice been recognized in the honorable mention section of the Best American Sports Writing series, and by the Associated Press Sports Editors and U.S. Basketball Writers Association. He graduated from Saint Joseph's University in Philadelphia with a degree in political science, and a minor in English. He lives in his hometown of Cranford, New Jersey, with his wife Amanda, daughter Quinn, and dog, Winnie. This is his first book.